THE PORTFOLIO PLANNER

MAKING PROFESSIONAL PORTFOLIOS WORK FOR YOU

Debra Bayles Martin
San Diego State University

Merrill,
an imprint of Prentice Hall
Upper Saddle River, New Jersey   Columbus, Ohio

Editor: Debra A. Stollenwerk
Production Editor: Julie Peters
Cover Designer: Diane C. Lorenzo
Production Manager: Pamela Bennett

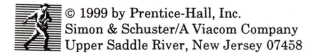

© 1999 by Prentice-Hall, Inc.
Simon & Schuster/A Viacom Company
Upper Saddle River, New Jersey 07458

Printed in the United States of America

10 9 8 7 6 5 4 3 2

ISBN: 0-13-081314-1

For Luke, always . . .

ACKNOWLEDGMENTS

Special thanks to:

Stacy Vinge for her generosity of spirit, her inquiring nature, and her enthusiasm for life and learning;

Debbie Stollenwerk for her vision and support;

The students who bring so much to our educational interactions;

The professionals who maintain a vision of student-centered classrooms and teacher-centered preparation programs.

*The purpose of education
is to allow each individual to come
into full possession of his or her personal power.*

—John Dewey

PREFACE

In the mid-1980s, many elementary students were enamored with the *Choose-Your-Own Adventure* fiction series (Bantam). Participating with the author by choosing how the story would progress personalized the reading experience in a unique way. Little did we know then that those books functioned as a sort of low-tech version of hypertext—allowing readers to enter and exit a storyline from any number of vantage points.

In many ways, my experiences with portfolios mirror those *Choose-Your-Own Adventure* stories. Like others, I have entered the world of professional portfolios from many vantage points, seen countless uses and abuses of the concept, and observed numerous twists and turns as applications are advanced, adopted, and altered.

This brief guide on professional portfolio planning is addressed primarily to preservice and inservice teachers. Because your professional portfolio needs will vary according to your context, perhaps portfolio planning might best be addressed through an electronic format—allowing you to "click" on particular hot links to visit websites of interest. However, even in this world of high-tech applications, there's still much to be said for the low-tech variety of choosing one's reading adventure with a text you can tuck into a bag or a pocket.

To support your reading, this book is organized in a format similar to the *Choose-Your-Own Adventure* paperback series. Throughout the pages, you'll see the "Cool Links" symbol. It will function like an electronic "hot link"—guiding you to other locations in the book where related concepts are discussed. "Cool Links" will allow you to personalize your journey so you can travel across and through the material according to your interests and questions.

From time to time, you'll also see "Teacher Thoughts" boxes. The comments in these boxes were written by practicing teachers in response to questions about their experiences with professional portfolios. Their observations highlight some strengths of professional portfolio development, as well as some pitfalls.

A third feature of this guide results from interactions with Stacy Vinge, a first-grade teacher in the San Diego area and a graduate student in the Reading Master's Program at San Diego State University. Stacy graciously consented to share her thoughts about professional portfolio development, along with some of the artifacts she has collected during her teaching career.

One way to begin your journey through this guide is to turn to the Key Questions on page 10 and peruse the topics there. If something catches your attention, follow the text and the "Cool Links" as far as you'd like. At any juncture, you can return to the Key Questions page to begin other journeys.

If the *Choose-Your-Own Adventure* approach doesn't appeal to you, a Table of Contents appears on page 8. You'll note that the book is organized into three major sections. In Section One, discussions center on common questions about professional portfolios. Each discussion has been designed to stand independently, or you can read the discussions in order.

Section Two includes Portfolio Planning Guides to help you create professional portfolios for different audiences and purposes. You can use these pages as checklists for developing particular portfolios, or they can serve as brainstorming prompts to help you customize your own portfolio guide.

Finally, Section Three provides text and media references to guide you to other professional portfolio adventures.

Whether you're interested in completing a teacher preparation program, documenting your professional growth, or addressing another purpose, I hope you'll enjoy co-creating at least part of your journey within the pages of this text.

—Debra Bayles Martin

CONTENTS

SECTION ONE

COMMON QUESTIONS ABOUT PROFESSIONAL PORTFOLIOS

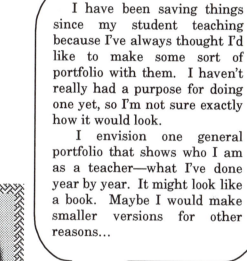

I have been saving things since my student teaching because I've always thought I'd like to make some sort of portfolio with them. I haven't really had a purpose for doing one yet, so I'm not sure exactly how it would look.

I envision one general portfolio that shows who I am as a teacher—what I've done year by year. It might look like a book. Maybe I would make smaller versions for other reasons...

KEY QUESTIONS FOR READING THIS BOOK

If you would like to read this book by topics, select one of the questions below and follow the Cool Link to the listed page. You can also proceed straight through the book, beginning with the next page.

1. I've heard a lot about portfolios. But I'm wondering, **what is a professional portfolio**?

For descriptions and definitions of various types of portfolios, go to page 11.

2. I'm pretty comfortable with what a portfolio is, but I'd like to read more about **different purposes for professional portfolios**.

See pages 18, 21, 35, and 41, or Question 3 below.

3. I understand the general definition and purposes of portfolios. What I want to know is **how professional portfolios can be of use to me in my current setting.**

See pages 18, 25, or 44-46 if you are preparing to enter or are enrolled in a teacher preparation program.
See pages 25 or 48-53 if you are (or will be soon) seeking your first teaching position.
See pages 19, 26, or 47 if you are a graduate student in education.
See pages 25, 31-33, or 48-53 if you are an inservice teacher considering career advancement or development.

4. I already do a lot with portfolios. I want to think about **ways to improve what I already do with professional portfolios**.

See page 59 for five ideas to enhance portfolio use, and page 63 for a discussion of electronic portfolios.

WHAT IS A PROFESSIONAL PORTFOLIO?

Growth without documentation remains too private;
documentation without growth is too trivial.

—Glatthorn, 1996

While professional portfolios are relatively new to education, they have "an ancient and honorable history" among artists, writers, and architects (Glatthorn, 1996, p. 31). For generations, professionals in these fields have collected samples of work to demonstrate their talent and skill. The idea of using portfolios to document teaching experience and expertise is rooted in these traditions. It is also supported by constructivist views of learning and over two decades of experimentation with student portfolios.

A series of education studies during the 1980s also encouraged the eventual use of professional portfolios. The 1983 federal report, "A Nation at Risk," stirred public concern about American education. Calls for enhanced student learning and increased teacher accountability rose from all sides. One of the most influential reform suggestions appeared in the 1986 Carnegie Corporation report, "A Nation Prepared: Teachers for the 21st Century." Report writers suggested that greater educational accountability could be achieved by redefining the role of teachers. Instead of someone who efficiently dispenses facts to students, the ideal teacher would be "flexible, up-to-date, [and] able to *lead* children into deeper learning" (*Teaching as a Profession*, 1997, p. 2, emphasis added).

During the past decade, increasing numbers of educators and researchers have embraced a view of learning which resonates with the Carnegie vision of teaching as active and learner-centered (Wolf & Siu-Runyan, 1996). This perspective is often referred to as a constructivist view. Constructivists believe that children build (construct) their own understanding of the world by using what they already know to interpret new ideas and experiences. These interpretations then become part of the child's ever-growing knowledge base.

If children are creators of their own knowledge, then teachers ideally become facilitators of learning rather than transmitters of information. A constructivist teacher functions more like a coach—helping children become aware of the world around them, encouraging them to think about how new ideas and experiences

3

relate to what they already know, and inviting them to take increasing responsibility for their conclusions and actions.

A constructivist view of teaching and learning requires much more of teachers than to simply take in a collection of facts from teacher preparation courses and then present that information to children. Indeed, as Anderson (1997) notes, teaching is, "at its core, a moral act" which requires careful thought and action (p. 2). To facilitate learning, constructivist teachers must know their students and their backgrounds, understand how knowledge is defined in various disciplines, consider contexts under which learning may best occur—and then orchestrate educational conditions to encourage optimum student growth. Such teachers become "lifelong learners seeking professional development" (Anderson, 1997, p. 2).

Constructivist views emphasize not only what teachers *know*, but what they *do*. Since much of what a teacher knows and actually does in a classroom is not easily measured with traditional paper/pencil assessments, other means of documenting teacher performance are being explored. With ever-increasing frequency, the professional portfolio is surfacing as a popular tool for documenting teacher preparation, inservice performance, and professional development (Bradley, 1997a; Cooper, 1997).

While the idea of collecting samples of one's work to document teaching experience and expertise may seem simple, a quick glance at the professional literature or a brief search on the Internet reveals a seemingly endless array of portfolio names, types, and purposes. This can lead to confusion about what someone means when they refer to a "professional portfolio."

When they hear the term "professional portfolio," some people think of an enhanced resumé. This is probably because professional portfolios are sometimes connected with job interviews and career advancement. Others envision scrapbooks filled with lesson plans, teaching evaluations, and photos of students engaged in classroom projects. Because our knowledge and use of professional portfolios draws heavily from what we have learned in using portfolios with elementary and secondary students over the past twenty years, it is helpful to compare student portfolios with their professional counterparts.

4

Comparing Student Portfolios to Professional Portfolios

Murnane (1994) defines a student portfolio as a "multidimensional collection of a student's work assembled in an organized fashion" where "specific attention is given to what students are doing and can do" (p. 74). Paris and Ayres (1994) add that portfolio-building involves a *process* as much as a *product*, since work samples should be collected and reviewed in "a systematic way" (p. 167).

McLaughlin and Vogt (1996) expand the idea of *process* to include collaboration between student and teacher as portfolio samples are selected and organized. Porter and Cleland (1995) add that portfolio selections should be "accompanied by a reflective narrative that not only helps the learner to understand and extend learning, but invites the reader of the portfolio to gain insight about learning and the learner" (p. 154).

From these ideas we can describe a student portfolio as a two-part experience. The first part of the experience involves students in collecting samples of their work over time and considering what those samples demonstrate (often with the aid of peer and instructor feedback). The second part of the experience involves deciding which samples best illustrate important insights, accomplishments, or values; considering how those samples (and insights) might best be presented to an audience; and then creating an actual presentation product. Students can engage in a portfolio process for a number of different reasons (e.g., to examine their progress in a subject area and set goals for further work, to demonstrate competency in a certain field), and they can tailor their presentation products to any number of audiences (e.g., themselves, teachers, parents, administrators).

Teachers have discovered many benefits from engaging students in portfolio-building. According to Young, Mathews, Kietzmann & Westerfield (1997), some of the most prominent include:

- Documenting growth in learning or increased proficiency in a particular area over time.
- Documenting growth that is not easily assessed through more traditional means such as standardized tests and application forms.
- Enhancing a learner's ownership of learning.
- Encouraging learner reflection on past experiences as well as in determining future learning goals.
- Involving participants in inquiry.

- Enhancing relationships among portfolio creators and mentors.
- Encouraging a sense of community and cooperation among learners rather than a sense of competition.
- Allowing individuals to display learning in ways overlooked or undervalued by other assessment means.
- Increasing involvement in writing, in discussions, and in interactions with other professionals.

Given the benefits of portfolio-building among young students, many educators and administrators have wondered if engaging teacher preparation students and practicing professionals in portfolio development might yield similar benefits. This leads to the question of how and when adults might build their own portfolios.

Creating a Professional Portfolio: Process and Product

Based on what we know about the portfolio process for younger students, creating a professional portfolio[1] involves going through a systematic *process* to create a particular *product* to address a particular audience or to achieve a specific goal. Although the *product* of a portfolio process may function somewhat like an enhanced resumé (if the creator's goal is to demonstrate particular achievements), the portfolio *process* itself is much broader than simply listing an academic or employment history. Job-seeking is only one of many reasons individuals create professional portfolios.

 See page 18 for more on goals for creating professional portfolios.

Like building a student portfolio, developing a professional portfolio means engaging in a *process* that results in a tangible *product*. This process involves five steps. First, you select a personal or professional goal (such as graduation, certification, professional advancement). Second, you think about how your professional experiences relate to that goal. Third, you collect actual items and

---

[1] For this discussion, "professional" refers to anyone engaged in professional preparation at the undergraduate or graduate level, as well as to practicing educators. "Professional portfolios" can be created at any time during a career, from its beginning in teacher preparation programs throughout advanced study and inservice practice.

documents[2] that could demonstrate what you have done (or are doing) to reach your goal.[3] Fourth, you decide which items among your collection best illustrate your achievement of or progress toward the goal. Finally, you determine how to present the selected items to the individual or group connected with your goal (e.g., instructor, evaluation committee, personnel director). All of these steps can be completed on your own, or with the aid and input of others (e.g., peers, colleagues, mentors).

As a result of going through the five steps above, you create a *product* which includes only the items you feel best illustrate specific accomplishments. Generally, you also share your reasons for selecting the items by including a written reflection with the finished portfolio *product*. These reflections are intended to help a portfolio reader gain insight into the *process* behind the *product*.

The "multidimensional" aspect of portfolio *products* requires us to make important decisions about what to collect and how to best present our selections. For example, is a teaching portfolio designed for career advancement best housed in a folder, a three-ring binder, a plastic file box, or in an electronic format? Should the product include students' drawings and papers created during a unit of study? Is it better to include three-dimensional objects (e.g., a student's clay sculpture) or to rely on photos and narrative descriptions? Should a teaching approach be described in writing or is it preferable to include a videotape of a particular teaching event?

Obviously, the nature of a professional portfolio (*process* and *product*) will vary according to its central purpose (Wolf & Siu-Runyan, 1996). Any time you consider creating a professional portfolio, there are several questions you should ask yourself. These questions appear on the next two pages. Each question includes a "Cool Link" to direct you to related material in this book.

---

[2] Because they range from two-dimensional pictures and papers to three-dimensional items such as videotapes and art projects, many writers refer to these samples as **artifacts**. For our discussion, "**artifact**" will refer to any item you could collect to demonstrate what you are learning or doing as a professional. This includes samples of your students' work as well.

[3] Some refer to the complete collection of items from which you will select certain samples as a "**working portfolio**." See page 38 for a discussion on working portfolios.

1. Why am I creating a professional portfolio?

Your central purpose or goal for creating a professional portfolio probably depends upon your situation. Turn to Question 3 on page 10 and select from the Cool Links the situation that most closely relates to your current context.

2. What will I include in my portfolio?

Check out the **Portfolio Planning Guides** beginning on page 73 for lists of possible items to include in different types of portfolios.

3. When will I collect and organize the samples and artifacts for the portfolio product?

Check out the **Portfolio Planning Pages** beginning on page 73 for ideas on time frames for collection.

4. How will I display and present my collection?

The **Portfolio Planning Guides** beginning on page 73 include ideas about different portfolio containers. You may also want to read about electronic portfolios beginning on page 63.

5. Who am I as a learner and who am I sharing this portfolio with?

Turn to page 41 to read about the value of reflection as part of the portfolio process. You can also go to pages 21-24 to consider various audiences for your portfolio.

6. Who might help me select or review the contents of my portfolio?

Turn to pages 38, 44, or 48 for some ideas on selecting portfolio artifacts. You may also want to go to page 42 for thoughts on sharing your work with others.

7. Where is this portfolio going and how can my choices best facilitate that journey?

This question is particularly important if you're working with an electronic portfolio that you plan to put on the Internet. See page 63 for some thoughts on electronic portfolios. The "container" suggestions on each **Planning Guide** (beginning with page 73) will also provide ideas.

WHY CREATE A PROFESSIONAL PORTFOLIO?

... If carefully conceptualized, portfolios not only present a window on learning but also promote growth....

—Wolf & Siu-Runyan, 1996

One of the portfolio's greatest strengths is its adaptability; you can collect a group of artifacts over any period of time and present them to an audience for almost any purpose. However, since the experience can be very time-consuming, it makes sense to create a professional portfolio only when you feel it is the best way to address a particular goal.

Generally speaking, goals for creating professional portfolios usually arise from your setting. For example, if you're a university student, you may create a professional portfolio because it is required by the course instructor. In this case, the materials you collect and the format in which you present them may be outlined for you. While you will likely reap many benefits from creating a course portfolio, your main goal for doing so is probably to achieve course credit by demonstrating your understanding of course content. At the beginning of the semester, your answers to the seven portfolio planning questions (from pages 16-17) might look something like this:

1. **Why am I creating a professional portfolio?**
   To achieve course credit.
2. **What will I include in my portfolio?**
   My instructor requires a sample lesson plan, three essays about teaching, and one "free choice" entry.
3. **When will I collect and organize the samples and artifacts for the portfolio product?**
   I will create and collect the samples during the semester and organize them during the last week of classes. The portfolio is due during finals week.
4. **How will I display and present my collection?**
   My instructor suggested that we use a three-ring binder to collect paper materials. She also said that if we included a videotape of ourselves teaching a small group of students, we should use a binder with a pocket big enough to hold the video.

5. **Who am I as a learner and who am I sharing this portfolio with?**

   I've never thought about who I am as a learner before. I'm not even sure what it means. I think the professor is the only one who'll see my portfolio, although maybe some of the other students in the class will share ideas.

6. **Who might help me select or review the contents of my portfolio?**

   My course instructor has told us what to include for most of the items. Maybe I could also ask the teacher I'm observing what he thinks I should include. I'll also talk with other students in the class to find out what they're doing for the "free choice" entry.

7. **Where is this portfolio going and how can my choices best facilitate that journey?**

   As far as I know it's just going to my professor. She said it's okay to include video or audio tapes. I'll have to think about whether I'm going to do that.

If you're about to graduate from a teacher education program (undergraduate or graduate), you may be developing a portfolio as part of graduation requirements. In this case, you're probably selecting items to represent what you have learned across many courses. Just as with a portfolio created for a single university course, criteria for your graduation portfolio will probably be outlined for you—perhaps based on specific program guidelines or on teaching standards.

 See pages 44-47 for ideas on academic portfolios designed to address entire programs of study.
A discussion of portfolios and teaching standards begins on page 25.

As you can tell, each professional portfolio is tailored to a specific purpose and audience. While you may create a general teaching portfolio for job interviews (or for introducing yourself to parents and students), you may also decide to create other portfolios during your professional career. One way to think about the kinds of portfolios you can create is to consider the major context in which they are developed. For most educators, professional portfolios arise: 1) as part of a formal **academic** setting (such as a university course), or 2) in connection with **professional development** sites (e.g., classroom, school, district).

Academic and Professional Advancement Portfolios

Academic portfolios are created as part of structured, formal courses or programs of study (e.g., teacher preparation courses, graduate programs). Such portfolios are usually implemented for the same reasons portfolios are used with younger children—to involve adults more actively in their learning.

 See page 44 for more extended discussion on academic portfolios, and pages 78 and 80 for related **Portfolio Planning Guides**.

In contrast, **professional development** portfolios are usually created to address questions or goals *outside* of the university classroom. Educators use professional development portfolios to explore and solve classroom challenges, extend their teaching expertise, and advance in their careers (e.g., achieve mentor teacher status or gain tenure).

 See page 48 for more extended discussion on professional development portfolios, and pages 82 and 84 for related **Portfolio Planning Guides**.

Although we can categorize professional portfolios according to their general setting and purpose, sometimes the categories intersect. For example, a teacher who is working on an advanced degree in education may complete an academic portfolio for a Reading Methods class at the university. However, if he explored and implemented reading intervention strategies with struggling readers in his classroom, he is growing professionally as well. Using the same information (e.g., list of reading strategies, measures of student progress), he could direct a portfolio product to his college instructor (academic portfolio) or to his school district to be considered for tenure or another advancement (professional development portfolio).

Beyond the Portfolio Creator: Other Reasons to Create a Professional Portfolio

While one goal of professional portfolios is to enhance teacher growth and development, there are other reasons for professional portfolio use. Just as teachers can use student portfolios to inform curriculum decisions, so too can university instructors, personnel directors, licensure boards, and others use them to help make various judgments and decisions.

When a portfolio is used as a tool to encourage personal growth rather than as a device to evaluate and rank individuals in a more competitive way, related decisions are usually "low-stakes" in nature. "Low-stakes" decisions are those that tend to benefit all participants. For example, let's suppose a principal asks all of the teachers in her school to create a professional portfolio centered on a successful classroom intervention. The teachers collect artifacts to demonstrate their use of a particular strategy, reflect on their teaching and its outcomes, and present their professional portfolios to one another at the end of the school year.

During the sharing, each teacher can celebrate his or her achievements and see what other faculty members have been doing. Informed by the teachers' portfolios, the principal can plan future inservice training to take advantage of staff strengths. She can also determine where future growth is needed. As in this example, low-stakes uses of portfolios provide important information for decision-making while still encouraging highly individual expression and an "everybody wins" attitude among participants.

However, professional portfolios can also be used in more "high-stakes" decision-making. In high-stakes decisions, some individuals receive a particular benefit over others, (e.g., college admission, job offers, career advancement opportunities). Many researchers suggest that it is counter-productive to use portfolios for such decisions (Doolittle, 1994; Glatthorn, 1996). In spite of such criticism, the current reality of professional portfolios includes high-stakes evaluation—from certifying preservice teachers for credentials to determining candidate qualifications for career advancement. Understanding potential power balances between portfolio submitters and administrators[4] can help us better address our portfolios to specific audiences.

Addressing Power Balances in Professional Portfolio Submission

The amount of input we have in a given portfolio submission process can provide important clues about our audience and their purposes for requiring portfolios. Let's examine three power balances that often exist between portfolio administrators and submitters: 1) High administrator control and low submitter input, 2) Low administrator control and high submitter input, and 3) Balanced control and input.

High Administrator Control. Administrators often maintain control of portfolio content and form when they are comparing candidates against one another (as in a job interview) or ranking them in some way. This is usually because allowing too much latitude results in portfolios so individualized that it's almost impossible to compare them. Controlling or standardizing all or part of the process ensures that candidates will address the same issues—allowing for comparison among individuals.

High administrative control can also occur when portfolio evaluation is being implemented for the first time. Often an administrator's first portfolio requirements will appear more

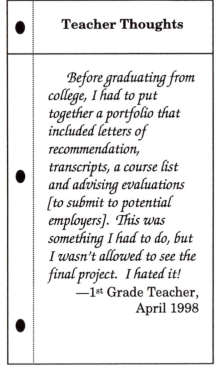

Teacher Thoughts

Before graduating from college, I had to put together a portfolio that included letters of recommendation, transcripts, a course list and advising evaluations [to submit to potential employers]. This was something I had to do, but I wasn't allowed to see the final project. I hated it!
—1st Grade Teacher, April 1998

---

[4]The term **"administrator"** will be used throughout the text to refer to someone who requires or "administers" portfolio assessment. This term is not meant to refer only to building and district administrative personnel—it can also apply to teachers who require portfolio submissions in their classes.

like a list of course assignments to be gathered rather than as an open-ended invitation to demonstrate learning (Stahle & Mitchell, 1993; Tierney, Carter, & Desai, 1991). If we are new to the process, we may appreciate very specific guidelines for portfolio submission. However, the reverse is also true—overly specific guidelines can be restrictive. It can be frustrating to select an artifact you feel truly demonstrates your expertise in an area, only to discover that it will not be accepted for evaluation. Like the first-grade teacher mentioned on page 22, the process also lacks appeal if its purposes are unclear or if too much control is withheld from the portfolio-builder.

If you are submitting a highly prescriptive portfolio, it will pay to follow the guidelines closely. This will aid evaluators in ranking your work. If you feel stifled by the criteria, you can still gain personal satisfaction from the process in at least two ways. First, focus on what you have learned and accomplished rather than on the format restrictions. Just because you can't submit a particular artifact for evaluation doesn't mean you shouldn't allow yourself to enjoy the memories associated with it!

Secondly, even in the most restrictive settings, you can usually achieve a uniquely personal presentation through the materials you select and how you put them together. Exercise your creativity by choosing interesting types and colors of paper on which you print portfolio entries, dividing portfolio sections in a certain way, using quotations or photos with section divisions, using borders and graphics, and in assuming a style and tone in your reflective writings and artifact captions.

 Reviewing the guides in **SECTION TWO** may fuel your thinking. A discussion on portfolio evaluation (page 54) also provides some ideas for portfolio formats.

Low Administrator Control. While some administrators using portfolio assessment for the first time adopt a highly prescriptive approach, others provide little or no guidance, perhaps because they are still grappling with the concept themselves. Open-ended portfolio guidelines allow us to take greater control of our professional portfolio contents and presentation. This can result in a delightful journey of exploration and discovery.

Unfortunately, the joy derived from taking greater control of the portfolio process is sometimes tempered with anxiety or frustration. In the absence of clear submission guidelines, we may wonder if there are items we are "supposed" to include in our portfolios, what evaluators are looking for, and whether evaluators will even look at our portfolios! "After all," we might find ourselves thinking, "if they don't tell us what they want, maybe they don't really want anything at all!"

If you've been given a great deal of control over your portfolio process and product, take some time to set evaluative criteria for yourself—so that you will be pleased with your efforts regardless of external feedback. If you're feeling anxious or concerned, request guidelines from the individual or institution. If these are not available, consider the likely purposes or goals behind the portfolio request. Why do you think this administrator has asked for professional portfolios? What is the individual or group seeking to evaluate, address, or achieve? Putting yourself in the shoes of your evaluator will help you find a more useful focus for your portfolio.

Balancing Power. In most cases, a balance of control and input between the administrator and the submitter is probably the most productive and satisfying for everyone. Basic guidelines help us form a mental image of what our audience hopes to see, while invitations for individual expression engage our creative, imaginative selves.

Professional portfolio submissions allow administrators and

Turn to page 54 for ideas on evaluating portfolios, and to page 38 for ideas about what to include in a portfolio.

submitters to experience the wonderful individuality inherent in portfolio development, and may also lead to important insights about program strengths and weaknesses or candidate interests and abilities. While achieving a balance between administrative control and submitter input will likely remain a challenge in every setting, the effort is well worth making (P. Roeder, personal communication, 17 April, 1998).

HOW DO PROFESSIONAL PORTFOLIOS RELATE TO TEACHING STANDARDS AND ACCOUNTABILITY?

- *What teachers know and can do is the most important influence on what students learn.*
- *Recruiting, preparing, and retaining good teachers is the central strategy for improving our schools.*
- *School reform cannot succeed unless it focuses on creating the conditions in which teachers can teach, and teach well.*

—National Commission on Teaching and America's Future, 1996

Because they believe teacher quality is central to education reform, many education-minded groups have proposed sets of standards in the past few years designed to improve teacher preparation and professional development opportunities. These standards or related improvement efforts generally fall into one of three categories:

1. Defining the roles and responsibilities of **teacher preparation institutions** (including student recruitment, assessment, and retention);
2. Setting standards for **beginning teachers** (initial certification or licensure, support in moving from the teacher preparation program into the profession); and
3. Enhancing **ongoing professional development for practicing teachers** (with teachers moving beyond standards set for beginning teachers—including renewable licensure and advanced board certification).

While recommendations and actions in each of these categories differ according to the originating group and its purposes (e.g., state or national legislatures, academic consortia, local district review committees) one theme appears in all of the work. That theme is an emphasis not only on what teachers *know*—but on what they *do*.

Just as classroom teachers have become increasingly interested in performance assessment for their students, so other educational stakeholders have begun to focus on performance assessment of teachers. Related to each of the three areas above we are seeing at both the state and national level: a) attempts to attract and retain more qualified candidates to the teaching profession, b) recommendations for minimum competency requirements for various "levels" of the teaching profession, and c) efforts to assess teacher knowledge and skill through means other than paper and pencil assessment.

One way to organize these reforms and the sets of standards that have developed over time is to think about them in three categories: 1) Reforms related to teacher preparation, 2) Reforms related to beginning teacher certification and licensure, and 3) Reforms related to the professional growth and development of practicing teachers.

Reforms Related to Teacher Preparation Programs

As researchers, policymakers, and others have redefined what it means to be a teacher, the institutions where teachers are prepared have come under increased scrutiny. Concerns have centered on the quality of candidates who enter teacher preparation programs and the effectiveness of the teacher preparation programs themselves.

Teacher Education Candidates. Believing that academically strong students will become better teachers, some policymakers have raised academic requirements for entry into and graduation from their education programs. While traditional measures such as test scores and grade point average are part of the more rigorous admission standards, an increasing number of education programs are also reviewing candidate potential by reading personal essays, reviewing portfolios, and even interviewing candidates.

If you are applying for admission to a teacher preparation or advanced educational degree program, you'll want to check out your institution's admission standards and consider how you can best demonstrate your academic competencies. Include in your application materials references to your involvement in areas such as student government, community service, and children's organizations. Describe what you have done in these settings that informs your view of teaching and enhances your ability to share ideas and create excellent learning environments. You may want to begin now to collect materials for a portfolio submission if your intended program requires one.

 You'll find a **Portfolio Planning Guide for Admission to a Program of Study** on page 78.

In addition to raising academic standards for teacher preparation programs, other reforms designed to attract quality candidates to the teaching profession include providing incentives for selecting education as a profession (such as forgivable loans), intern programs (in which education students receive a partial or complete salary during a special full-time student-teaching experience), and mentoring programs to help first-year teachers make the transition to full-time teaching. Whereas all of these steps may be important and helpful for recruiting excellent candidates as future teachers, they are ill-advised if teacher preparation programs lack quality and meaning. As a result, reforms have also focused on teacher certification programs.

Teacher Preparation Programs. Much of the concern about educational reform has found voice in the form of standards—standards which describe what a beginning teacher should know and be able to do. With the role of a beginning teacher outlined, teacher preparation programs can be examined for their effectiveness in helping students achieve specific teaching standards.

For beginning teachers, the Interstate New Teacher Assessment and Support Consortium (INTASC) Standards are probably the most well-known. These standards were developed in 1990 by The Council of Chief State School Officers, a consortium of leaders from thirty states. In 1995, the INTASC standards were revised and published—and have been adopted in whole or in part by a number of states as guides for revamping teacher certification and licensure procedures.

The INTASC Standards consist of ten brief statements which describe what a beginning teacher should know and be able to do. These statements appear in Figure 1.

Standard	Explanation
1. Knowledge of subject	The teacher understands the central concepts, tools of inquiry, and structures of the discipline(s) he or she teaches and can create learning experiences that make these aspects of subject matter meaningful for students.
2. Learning and human development	The teacher understands how children learn and develop and can provide learning opportunities that support their intellectual, social, and personal development.
3. Adapting instruction	The teacher understands how students differ in their approaches to learning and creates instructional opportunities that are adapted to diverse learners.
4. Strategies	The teacher understands and uses a variety of instructional strategies to encourage students' development of critical thinking, problem solving, and performance skills.
5. Motivation and management	The teacher uses an understanding of individual and group motivation and behavior to create a learning environment that encourages positive social interaction, active engagement in learning, and self-motivation.
6. Communication skills	The teacher uses knowledge of effective verbal, nonverbal, and media communication techniques to foster active inquiry, collaboration, and supportive interaction in the classroom.
7. Planning	The teacher plans instruction based upon knowledge of subject matter, students, the community, and curriculum goals.
8. Assessment	The teacher understands and uses formal and informal assessment strategies to evaluate and ensure the continuous intellectual, social, and physical development of the learner.
9. Commitment	The teacher is a reflective practitioner who continually evaluates the effects of his/her choices and actions on others (students, parents, and other professionals in the learning community) and who actively seeks out opportunities to grow professionally.
10. Partnerships	The teacher fosters relationships with school colleagues, parents, and agencies in the larger community to support students' learning and well-being.

Figure 1 INTASC Model Standards for Beginning Teachers
(*Source*: http://develop.ccsso-cybercentral.com/nextstep.htm)

Because the INTASC standards include a performance aspect (what a teacher can *do*), it is difficult to determine whether a beginning teacher meets them without implementing some form of performance-based assessment. In many states, candidates develop professional portfolios to demonstrate their understanding and application of INTASC standards in the classroom as part of the teacher certification process.

 A number of websites and professional books address using specific standards for developing portfolios. The book by Campbell, et al., (1997) is devoted specifically to addressing INTASC standards, and is referenced on page 92.

Because increasing numbers of beginning teachers will probably be asked to address the INTASC standards (or something similar), teacher educators are revising course requirements to include more active learning and performance-based assessment. This is not to suggest that INTASC standards have been the major impetus for changes in teacher education programs. For some time, teacher educators have experimented with various approaches to teacher preparation to encourage reflection, inquiry, and collaboration among their students.

In the meantime, the National Council for Accreditation of Teacher Education (NCATE) has incorporated the INTASC standards into its criteria for evaluating teacher education programs. Such inclusion is a significant step, because this voluntary accrediting body accredits about 500 institutions in education and related fields (Bradley, 1997b). It also represents a significant shift in focus. In the past, NCATE evaluators relied mainly on descriptions of teacher preparation programs and student achievement to determine whether a program should be accredited. By the year 2000, NCATE will evaluate teacher preparation programs not only through traditional means, but also by exploring how well an institution's graduates actually teach. While they won't actually observe education program graduates teaching, it's possible that national accreditation teams may routinely look at student portfolios as "one way to judge the quality of a program under review" (Bradley, 1997c, p. 2).

Already, several states have implemented or are experimenting with performance-based requirements for beginning teacher certification. It is unlikely that in the future, individuals will not automatically receive state certification upon completion of an accredited education program. Rather, the licensing process will probably mirror that of medicine and law—where candidates must pass a statewide competency exam before practicing in their profession.

Because of the current emphasis on the application of teacher knowledge, teacher certification procedures will probably continue to include a performance component. Although portfolio assessment is not the only type of performance-based measure available, it is popular with present policymakers. Since a quality portfolio requires some time to produce, it is wise to find out near the beginning of your teacher preparation program what standards you may be expected to address upon graduation to demonstrate your professional competency as a beginning teacher. So informed, you can collect artifacts from the beginning of your program into a working portfolio. Later, you can select artifacts that best document your professional preparation achievements to create a certification portfolio.

 A **Planning Guide for a Certification Portfolio** appears on page 80. See page 38 for more on working portfolios.

Even if your institution does not currently require portfolios, it is possible that it may in the future. If you are selecting a teacher preparation program, you may want to consider how your intended program addresses not only your state's standards for teacher education, but also whether national standards play a role in the way your program unfolds. You may also want to investigate how your institution supports its graduates in the certification and licensure process.

 For a list of questions to help you evaluate teacher education programs, you can visit NCATE's website at: http://www.ncate.org/wannabe/lookfor.html

Reform Efforts and Standards for Ongoing Teacher Certification and Professional Development

Once someone completes a teacher preparation program and obtains a state certification or license, he or she ideally continues on a path of professional development that spans a lifetime. Cognizant of this fact, current education reform efforts also focus on how teachers grow professionally after they attain initial certification.

To ease the transition into full-time teaching, many universities, states, and school districts have devised programs to support beginning teachers. These programs generally involve new teachers in regular meetings where they problem-solve, learn about new instructional strategies, and reflect on their practice. The development (or enhancement) of a professional portfolio often accompanies these programs. This portfolio focus is seen as a way to help beginning teachers organize their growing knowledge about teaching.

Ideally, reformers envision at least a three-phase professional progression where teachers: 1) are active learners during their preparation programs, 2) achieve beginning teacher status, and 3) continue active inquiry about teaching throughout their profession, earning advanced professional certification(s) over time. The professional portfolio can be a common link across these experiences, representing a consistent approach toward thinking, learning, and sharing.

To encourage continued professional development (beyond initial certification), groups such as the National Board for Professional Teaching Standards (NBPTS) are implementing suggestions for documenting and assessing professional expertise among teachers with three or more years of teaching experience.

National Board for Professional Teaching Standards (NBPTS)

Established in 1987 as a result of recommendations in the Carnegie Task Force document "A Nation Prepared: Teachers for the 21st Century," the National Board for Professional Teaching Standards (NBPTS) is governed by a 63-member board of directors, the majority of whom are classroom teachers. The mission of the NBPTS (1997) encompasses three major goals:

> ...to establish high and rigorous standards for what accomplished teachers should know and be able to do, to develop and operate a national, voluntary system to assess and certify teachers who meet these standards, and to advance related education reforms for the purpose of improving student learning in American schools. (p. 1)

NBPTS certification is voluntary and is intended to symbolize professional teaching excellence. However, it is not designed to replace state licensure efforts, especially because most state efforts are directed toward certifying *beginning* teachers. National certification is intended to complement other certification efforts.

Similar to the ten INTASC standards, the National Board lists five core propositions as its focus. These propositions are listed in Figure 2:

1) Teachers are committed to students and their learning.
   a) Teachers recognize individual differences in their students and adjust their practice accordingly.
   b) Teachers have an understanding of how students develop and learn.
   c) Teachers treat students equitably.
   d) Teachers' mission extends beyond developing the cognitive capacity of their students.
2) Teachers know the subjects they teach and how to teach those subjects to students.
   a) Teachers appreciate how knowledge in their subjects is created, organized and linked to other disciplines.
   b) Teachers command specialized knowledge of how to convey a subject to students.
   c) Teachers generate multiple paths to knowledge.
3) Teachers are responsible for managing and monitoring student learning.
   a) Teachers call on multiple methods to meet their goals.
   b) Teachers orchestrate learning in group settings.
   c) Teachers place a premium on student engagement.
   d) Teachers regularly assess student progress.
   e) Teachers are mindful of their principal objectives.
4) Teachers think systematically about their practice and learn from experience.
   a) Teachers are continually making difficult choices that test their judgment.
   b) Teachers seek the advice of others and draw on education research and scholarship to improve their practice.
5) Teachers are members of learning communities.
   a) Teachers contribute to school effectiveness by collaborating with other professionals.
   b) Teachers work collaboratively with parents.
   c) Teachers take advantage of community resources.

Figure 2 Five core propositions of the National Board for Professional Teaching Standards

National Teacher Certification is offered in the following areas:

- Early Childhood/Generalist
- Middle Childhood/Generalist
- Early Adolescence/Generalist
- Early Adolescence/English Language Arts
- Adolescence and Young Adulthood/Mathematics
- Early Adolescence through Young Adulthood/Art

If you decide to apply for national certification, you'll prepare a portfolio to show evidence of good teaching practices and take a day-long written examination. The NBPTS notes that portfolio preparation generally requires at least 120 hours of work over 4-5 months. While the portfolio requirements differ according to the grade and subject matter specialization of the candidate, they generally require the following:

- Four to five classroom-based exercises (may include videotape of classroom interaction or discussion)
- Collection of particular student work
- Written analysis of the teaching reflected in the videotape or student work
- Documentation of the teacher's work outside the classroom with families, colleagues, and the community—including what the accomplishment was and its importance

National certification was achieved by almost half of those who applied in 1996-97 (the first available year), suggesting that the portfolios and written experiences were evaluated by rigorous standards.

Professional Portfolios and Teaching Standards: Where From Here?

If current trends continue, teacher preparation and certification procedures may become more cohesive than they ever have been. Ideally, a vision of what it means to be a proficient teacher will be shared among preparation programs and state/national licensure boards. Teacher candidates would enter active, engaging preparation programs designed to encourage personal and collaborative inquiry—and they would continue the formal and informal learning processes throughout their careers. Individuals would progress from candidate status through "levels" of professional development, earning various certifications and/or credentials along the way. And of course, the true beneficiaries of all this standard-setting and certification would be the children—who are met daily in their classrooms by well-prepared, enthusiastic teachers.

The vision of shared standards is compelling, and professional portfolios will likely play a major role in articulating the links from teacher preparation through professional advancement. In many ways, this is an exciting time for educators. Never has so much attention from so many places focused on education. However, in some ways, the notoriety is disconcerting. On the heels of shared vision flows too often the spectre of widespread standardization and regulation. The questions of how national standards will be fairly interpreted across diverse settings is only one of many sure to surface. There will be much to learn about standard-setting and equitable certification processes in the next few years. Clearly, the benefits of current reforms must outweigh the costs if they are to help students and teachers reach beyond today's performance and draw forth tomorrow's potential.

HOW CAN PORTFOLIOS BE OF USE TO ME IN MY CURRENT SETTING?

Teachers must also keep portfolios, not only to model the process for students, but to grow themselves as readers and writers.

—Danielson, 1996 in Wilcox, 1997

Besides addressing the purposes and audiences mentioned on pages 18 and 24, portfolio-building offers you the opportunity to do something far too rare for most of us—take time to think about where you are and where you want to be. Through the process of considering what kind of portfolio to keep, for how long, and for whom, you can take greater control of your own academic and professional development where it matters most—at the source (Burke, 1996). No matter where you teach and learn, surely there are things you'd like to understand better. Your decision to develop a formal collection of information about a topic will help you review what you already know and do, as well as reveal areas to explore further. As you ponder and collect, you'll also discover (or perhaps rediscover) aspects of your academic and professional development that bring you great fulfillment.

A good starting place for creating any portfolio is within your own mind (Goodwin & Hensley, 1997). Take time to self-assess; consider what you have accomplished relative to your career goals. Think about what you'd like to achieve and how creating a portfolio might help you accomplish this. It may be helpful to fill out the **Portfolio Purpose Reflection Grid** on the next page to clarify what kind of portfolio you want to create and with whom it will be shared.

As you think and plan, it's a good idea to regularly record your thoughts about teaching and learning (perhaps once a week in a journal format—or at the end of the day at the bottom of your plan book). You may also want to attach post-it notes to items you feel reflect important aspects of your teaching. You can also keep dated notes in a small notebook set aside specifically for that purpose. Whatever your method, you'll probably find later that you want to include some of these ideas and items in a more focused portfolio.

Portfolio Purpose Reflection Grid

Instructions: Read each question and mark an X in the response column that best matches your answer. Write in your own responses if needed.

A	B	C	D	Questions
				1) Why am I thinking about creating a portfolio? a) To receive course credit. b) To complete a program of study. c) To advance in my career. d) To see what I've learned, reflect on my teaching, or solve a teaching problem.
				2) Who is this portfolio for? a) An instructor. b) An evaluator. c) An educational administrator. d) Myself.
				3) What media/dimensions will I use/include? a) Paper only. b) Paper and video/audiotape. c) Electronic only. d) Other combination.
				4) Where will this portfolio go/appear? a) My instructor or evaluator will see it. b) My peers will review it. c) It will be on the Internet. d) It will stay with me.
				5) How will I present my reflections? a) As instructed or required. b) With the reflections of others (e.g., peer reviews). c) With formal write-ups for each artifact or by section. d) Casually, with post-it notes on artifacts.
				6) How will I present my reflections? a) As instructed or required. b) With the reflections of others (e.g., peer reviews). c) With formal write-ups for each artifact or by section. d) Casually, with Post-It notes on artifacts

If your responses appear predominantly in response columns A-B, you'll probably want to create an academic portfolio. Responses in columns C-D suggest a professional development portfolio.

To learn more about academic portfolios, go to page 44. Turn to page 48 for information on professional development portfolios. You may also want to think about starting a working portfolio, as described on page 38.

Another important step throughout any portfolio process is to discuss your ideas periodically with a trusted mentor or group of colleagues. Discussion with others helps us clarify our goals and consider perspectives other than our own (Wolf & Siu-Runyan, 1996).

 Careful reflection about practice is a basic part of teacher research and professional growth. You may want to explore how reflection, research, and teaching can work together by reading the article by Carol & John Santa referenced on page 94. You may also want to turn to page 41 to read more about reflection and professional portfolios.

WHAT SHOULD I INCLUDE IN A PROFESSIONAL PORTFOLIO?

Not only is a portfolio a place to organize information, to demonstrate growth and development, and to make my thinking visible, but it also allows me to monitor and manage my own learning...I can see what I know and how I came to know it.

—Wilcox, 1997

Obviously, what you include in your portfolio depends upon the purpose of your portfolio and its audience. A good first step is to establish a place to collect things that may be useful in creating a more focused portfolio later. This "place" (and the items collected there) can be called a **working portfolio**. A working portfolio can be established anywhere you can safely collect and organize various artifacts related to your teaching career. Some people use a pocket file folder, others reserve a desk or file drawer, and still others set aside a large box for collecting materials. In these containers they place important papers such as their teaching credentials, special units of study, etc. They also add photos, models, student work, and other items they may want to use as examples of their teaching and learning.

Keeping everything in one place is a great idea. I have a lot of recommendation letters and pictures of my students together in a pocket folder, but other items are kind of scattered. Some are with applications I've done and some are in separate files. A central place to store things by date would be great. I'm thinking of a box with file folders. I could put all the items from one year in one folder and keep them in order. If I needed something, it would be right there.

It's a good idea to keep a notebook with your working portfolio. Whenever you add an artifact, take a moment to note the date you added it (or the date it was attained) as well as the reason you saved it. If you're using file folders, note where the item is filed. You should also list events that do not generate artifacts. Without such a list, you may later overlook accomplishments or important events that contributed to your professional growth.

Ideally, you should begin collecting materials for your working portfolio from the beginning of your professional career and continue to its close. From this master collection you'll be able to select and present various artifacts for different purposes—as needed. If you're already teaching, you can begin now to collect items into a working portfolio. Over time you'll probably run across items from your student teaching and other settings and you can add them to the collection. The important step is to establish a master collection site and plan—NOW!

When you decide to create a smaller, more focused portfolio from your working portfolio, you'll probably want to include the following items, no matter what the specific focus:

- A title page or introduction, stating the theme and/or purpose of your portfolio.
- An introduction of yourself (and your students, if applicable) that personalizes your portfolio and helps your reader become acquainted with you. Your introduction can include items such as a resumé, a photo, a short written description of yourself and how you fulfill particular roles relevant to the reader/reviewer, and/or a brief philosophy statement about the particular area your portfolio is addressing.
- A way for your reviewer/reader to navigate your portfolio such as a table of contents or map of the portfolio.
- Samples of your work that demonstrate the traits/qualities you want to explore and/or share. (Limit the number of samples and be sure their connection to your portfolio focus is as clear as you can make it.)
- Some form of communication to the reader/viewer (such as a brief letter or written reflections) to explain why particular artifacts were selected for inclusion in the portfolio. This communication can appear once (perhaps near the beginning of your portfolio) or throughout the selections and should address why or how the examples and artifacts you have collected demonstrate your growth and/or abilities in a given area.
- Closing remarks thanking the reader/viewer for sharing your portfolio. (Some people like to include a way for readers to respond to the portfolio such as self-addressed stamped post cards

or electronic mail connections.) You may also want to inform the reader of how the portfolio can be returned to you (e.g., you will pick it up at a specific date and time).

Beyond the items listed above, what you include in your portfolio depends upon what you want to learn about (as in improving your classroom practice) or what you want to present to someone else (as in developing a portfolio to achieve a particular milestone). The planning guides in **SECTION TWO** have been compiled from many sources (Goodwin & Hensley, 1997; Klein, 1996; National Board for Professional Teaching Standards, 1997; Ross, 1997; Wagner, et al., 1994; Worchester, 1998) and include items that may be useful in developing portfolios for various purposes. As you read through the lists, let them serve as a point of departure for your own brainstorming. If you think of something else that demonstrates a particular achievement, include it!

Remember, professional portfolios are not scrapbooks or large collections of all you have accomplished (Bergeron, Wermuth & Hammar, 1997). Rather, they should include only a *few*, carefully chosen artifacts that you believe clearly demonstrate particular skills and knowledge for a specific audience and purpose. Haertel (1990) suggests using the value-added principle to guide your portfolio selections. Choose one piece of evidence to support a particular point. Before you include another item, ask yourself what it adds beyond the first piece. If the two are quite similar, it's likely that one piece will suffice.

Over time, you may actually develop several professional portfolios—for different purposes (Ross, 1997). Thus, when you review lists of possible portfolio artifacts, include only those items that best meet your goals for any one portfolio. <u>Don't try to put them all in</u>!

See page 88 for references to portfolio-related articles, books, and other media connections. While some of these resources focus on student portfolios, many of the ideas can be adapted to professional portfolios as well.

WHAT IS REFLECTION AND WHY IS IT OFTEN MENTIONED WITH PROFESSIONAL PORTFOLIOS?

Reflection is what allows us to learn from our experiences; it is an assessment of where we have been and where we want to be next.

—Wolf & Siu-Runyan, 1996

Today it seems that almost every proposal for educational reform lists professional development as the key to change (Guskey, 1994 in Cook, 1996). Just what is meant by professional development and how does it best occur?

For many years professional development has involved attending inservice presentations and conferences, or taking specific university courses. In both settings, presenters or instructors usually share ideas with a group of teachers who are encouraged to implement new concepts in their classrooms. Most of us have been through the experience—indeed, how often have you returned to your classroom aglow with anticipation, only to find the implementation of an idea neither as simple nor as effective as you expected? Where did you turn for help when faced with the "real" questions of change?

Obviously, teaching and learning are complex undertakings. Hearing about exciting ideas is only a beginning. The best way to engage in professional development and truly "get good at change" (Cook, 1996) involves taking the time to: 1) identify areas of challenge in our professional settings, 2) consider how we currently address these challenges, 3) explore options for change, and 4) experiment with various interventions over time—refining them until they become comfortable and effective (Bergeron, et al., 1997).

This careful, systematic consideration of practice is often called reflection. Reflective teachers constantly evaluate their goals and objectives, step back to look at their own teaching/learning performance, become keen observers of students (and other teachers), realize that student responses provide assessment information on a daily basis, and adjust their approaches to fit their situations (Paris & Ayres, 1994, p. 132). To be most effective, reflection should occur on a regular basis.

So how does a person go about reflecting? Glatthorn (1996) suggests six steps to the process:

1. Begin by becoming aware of your feelings, thoughts, teaching decisions, and student reactions.
2. Find a focus from the ideas you have noticed.
3. Seek to make sense of your focus through writing (perhaps using a regular journal entry technique).
4. Search for meaning in your writing and thinking.
5. Share your questions and insights with others.
6. Alter the behavior and begin a new cycle of reflection to review its results. (p. 27)

Sharing with others also helps us reflect (Rousculp & Maring, 1992). Unfortunately, sometimes as teachers we are reluctant to share personal development questions with our colleagues (Bergeron, et al., 1997) As you consider your setting and your questions, think of someone you like or admire. Try sharing a few ideas with that person in a casual way. You may be surprised at the results!

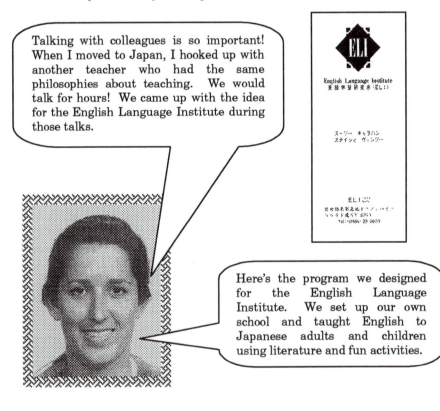

Talking with colleagues is so important! When I moved to Japan, I hooked up with another teacher who had the same philosophies about teaching. We would talk for hours! We came up with the idea for the English Language Institute during those talks.

Here's the program we designed for the English Language Institute. We set up our own school and taught English to Japanese adults and children using literature and fun activities.

Reflection should not focus only on things we accomplish or that go well. As Porter and Cleland (1995) remind us, reflection "can highlight not only what has been done, but what hasn't been done" (p. 39). Indeed, we often learn as much (or more) from things that don't go well as from things that do. Learning from our errors is another aspect of becoming reflective. Don't be afraid to examine your teaching from many sides—even the painful areas can contribute greatly to our professional growth if we face them head-on.

 Sometimes reflective pieces are so complete or instructive, they can be shared with a large audience. You may enjoy reading Elizabeth Meier Smith's (1992) reflection on her first teaching experience as an example. See page 95 for the reference.

WHAT GOES INTO AN ACADEMIC PORTFOLIO?

Practicing reflective thinking and new ways of knowing in a direct and focused way ensures that we learn from our own thoughtfulness.

—Wilcox, 1996

Portfolios have been used at the elementary level for some time. They've also been implemented in secondary schools and colleges, although on a smaller scale. Recently, the trend toward portfolio assessment has gained momentum among teacher education programs and graduate programs in reading (McLaughlin & Vogt, 1996; Smyser, 1994).

If you are asked to create a portfolio to document your academic progress in a college course or program, it's a good idea to find out whether the goal is to help you discover personal strengths and weaknesses and set goals for the future, or whether a more polished "best work" portfolio is desired. Read the submission guidelines closely and look for ways the portfolio will be evaluated—the more clearly you address the evaluation criteria, the more positive the experience will be for all involved.

 See pages 78-80 for related **Portfolio Planning Guides.** For more on evaluating portfolios, go to page 54.

ADMISSION TO A TEACHER PREPARATION PROGRAM

Because California requires a Bachelor's degree prior to enrollment in a teacher credential program, students interested in education often pursue a Liberal Studies undergraduate degree. At San Diego State University, the Liberal Studies program culminates with a portfolio submission where students demonstrate their understanding of various aspects of the Liberal Studies program and how they connect to the field of education. If you are preparing a portfolio for graduation from an undergraduate or graduate program, or for admission to a teacher preparation program, you may find some of the guidelines used at San Diego State University (SDSU) helpful in your own planning.

At SDSU, students are introduced to portfolio requirements when they enter the Liberal Studies major, and are encouraged to identify

36

and save specific course materials for future inclusion in their portfolios. Workshops are offered for juniors and seniors to provide more detail regarding portfolio development, and students are encouraged to work actively on their portfolios during their last two years of study. The finished portfolio is organized into two major sections: **Who You Are** and **What You Have Learned**.

The **Who You Are** section includes a personal resumé, and a brief personal history intended to introduce the author to the reader, explain his or her choice of a particular subject area specialization, and describe participation in extracurricular activities. A specific goal of this personal history is for students to describe how their life experiences have prepared them to become teachers. The **Who You Are** section also includes a values and attitudes essay, along with a capstone essay where students evaluate their experiences with the Liberal Studies program and with developing their professional portfolios.

In the **What You Have Learned** section, students include samples of their coursework from the program, each accompanied by a one-page reflection describing growth in a particular area and detailing how the artifact supports their comments. Additionally, students write an essay that connects ideas and information across two disciplines. This interdisciplinary focus helps students approach their learning from a more integrated perspective, preparing them to engage in developing thematic and integrated teaching units in the teacher preparation program.

In a similar vein, students at Miami University engage in a long-term portfolio building experience, including a genre-specific focus during their Freshman year (e.g., what I learned in my English course). They move to a goal-setting focus during their Sophomore and Junior years (what I want to learn based on what I see about myself as a learner so far). Finally, during their Senior year, they focus on creating a "best work" type portfolio, considering potential employers as their primary audience (McFadden, 1994).

Admission to Student Teaching: An Example from Alverno College

At Alverno College, students are asked to create a portfolio when seeking admission to student teaching. The goal of these portfolios is to provide "evidence" of readiness to student teach. Applicants are required to include in their portfolios the following:

- videotape of a lesson with children or young adults taught by the applicant.
- *written analysis of the videotaped lesson.*
- sample of work in subject area focus (e.g., area of specialization)
- a piece of reflective writing.
- *a sample of instructional materials created for teaching.*

As they examine portfolios, evaluators seek evidence that

 See page 38 for a discussion of a working portfolio, as well as the **Planning Guides** beginning on page 73 for some ideas about what to collect and include in various portfolios.

students integrate theory and practice, apply sound instructional principles, and are sensitive to diversity among students (Diez, 1994). Like the student portfolios at Alverno College, your portfolio will probably be more highly regarded if your written reflections are clear in their references to issues such as these.

In many places, university personnel are willing to respond to drafts of portfolio reflection papers. These responses provide helpful insight regarding program focus and ways to frame your ideas. If your university offers this kind of mentoring, take advantage of it—not only because it will help you create a stronger portfolio, but because you will gain insight into how your experiences and thinking relate to the teacher preparation program.

Just like the second-grade teacher suggests (p. 46), you

●	**Teacher Thoughts**

I wish I had had to do a portfolio in my credential program. I think a professional portfolio would be ideal for interviews or to parents who are concerned about who their child's teacher is. With everything that is going on in my life, it is hard to make a portfolio. Plus, if you start at the credential program level, you can have an ongoing portfolio. I think it is harder now to get one started because of lack of items from your early years.

—2nd Grade Teacher,
April 1998

may want to experiment with creating a portfolio, even if your current program doesn't require one. You can record field experiences and insights regularly in a journal, reflect on lesson activities (successes and failures), and collect materials you think may be useful in later career advancement.

Portfolios in Graduate Study

If you're a graduate student in an education-related field, you may experience portfolio development from a number of perspectives—possibly all at once. While this may seem overwhelming, you can use the experiences in one area to inform the other and enrich both.

For example, it is increasingly common for professors to ask graduate students to work with children (especially in literacy instruction) and develop a portfolio to illustrate the child's literacy progress. A companion portfolio documenting graduate student growth and insight is often assigned as well.

In many classes (both preservice and inservice) instructors are sharing with students examples of their own portfolios (Wilcox, 1996). If you are a student in such a course, don't be afraid to ask your instructor about his or her portfolio. You'll learn about your instructor and about portfolios through such experiences (Allen, 1996).

As you learn about others through portfolio sharing, you may want to explore related topics as part of your graduate research. For example, in comparing standardized test performance with portfolio assessment scores of more than 5,000 1st and 2nd grade students in New York, Educational Testing Service researchers recently found that "a student's gender explained significantly more of the variation in portfolio performance than it did of standardized-test performance, with girls performing significantly better than boys" (Supovitz, 1997, p. 2).

As you work through your portfolio experiences, you may want to investigate what types of reflection are most valued in portfolios and how these relate to the students with whom you interact. Clearly, you'll encounter endless research opportunities related to portfolio assessment—wherever and whenever it is used.

WHAT GOES INTO A PROFESSIONAL DEVELOPMENT PORTFOLIO?

Portfolios can facilitate professional growth as well as demonstrate it.

—Wilcox, 1996

A big part of professional development involves understanding how various individuals define the "role" of a teacher in a particular context and how you (as a teacher yourself) both reflect and challenge that role. In creating a portfolio for career advancement (first job or job change), consider how your employer envisions the "role" for which you are applying. Some aspects of the "role" are probably listed in the job descriptions and policy statements of a given school or district. If you take the time to "read between the lines," you'll probably discover some implicit role allusions as well. With this information, you can focus your portfolio contents and presentation to address how you fulfill and extend a given role.

If you are creating a professional development portfolio for a particular district or other institution, it is likely that you will receive guidelines regarding what your portfolio should address. These guidelines will probably encompass five areas:

1. Your educational philosophy.
2. What you have accomplished for professional development since receiving your teaching certificate.
3. How you define and address curriculum and instruction in your setting.
4. How you encourage and document student growth.
5. What non-teaching contributions you make to the school and to the community. (McLaughlin & Vogt, 1996, p. 99)

As you gather materials for a professional advancement portfolio, you may want to use these five categories as a filing guide. They can also prompt you to document particular accomplishments you might overlook (such as non-teaching contributions).

A professional portfolio can also be helpful in preparing for and going through professional interviews. As you review possible interview questions, you can set up your portfolio to help you respond to an interviewer and support your claims. While all interviewers will not be willing to peruse your portfolio during a screening interview, some may. Just in case, Goodwin and Hensley (1997) suggest that you note on your resumé that you can bring a portfolio to an interview.

As the first-grade teacher quoted here discovered, most personnel administrators and superintendents don't require portfolios from applicants, but principals may, especially because "more school officials are requesting them, finding that they provide important insight into a teacher's individual talents and beliefs about education" (Jacobson, 1997, p. 1).

If you are preparing for local interviews, the following list of common interview questions may help you think of ways to create a portfolio to support the interview process (Goodwin & Hensley, 1997; Larimer, 1998):

Teacher Thoughts

I put together a wonderful portfolio that included my resume, cover letter, self-made assessment and scoring, photos of special teaching ex-periences, credential and a few other things. Unfortunately, in every interview I've had, the interviewer seems reluctant to take my portfolio. The times I have left it, I don't think anyone has even looked at it. Basically, it was a lot of work that administrators and the human resource department don't have the time to look at.

—1st Grade Bilingual Teacher, April 1998

- Tell me a little bit about yourself.
- How would you describe yourself?
- What are your greatest strengths and weaknesses?
- Why did you select your college or university?
- Why did you choose your major?
- What are your career goals?
- Where do you see yourself five or ten years from now?
- How has your college experience prepared you for your career?
- What qualifications do you have that you think will make you successful in this position?
- Describe your most rewarding accomplishment.
- Describe a challenge you encountered and how you dealt with it.
- Why are you interested in working for our school or district?

- What do you know about our school/district?
- What two or three things are most important to you in your job?
- Why should I hire you?
- What key learning theory (or theories) guide your instructional design and decisions?
- How would you establish and maintain a healthy learning environment for your students?
- How would you involve parents and community members in your classroom? in our school? in our district?

Although these questions are framed for a student completing university training and entering the job market for the first time, you can adapt the same questions for employment at another stage of your career with slight modifications.

You may also want to consider the **P. A. R.** approach (Goodwin & Hensley, 1997) in preparing portfolio entries. To do this, select two or three instances for which you describe a **P**roblem you encountered, the **A**ction you took, and the **R**esults of that action.

For example, let's say that you wanted your students to read a particular novel as part of a history unit. Unfortunately, you only located five copies of the novel—even after visiting all the local libraries and bookstores. Because you were sure the novel would add to the unit, you sought the advice of colleagues and read through several professional journals and books. During your search, you found the "Read-a-Book-in-an-Hour" strategy, which allows you to share a novel with a whole class using only one copy (Bromley, 1992, p. 217). With this solution, you shared the book with your students and gathered their written responses to it. They loved the book and your unit was very successful. Your resulting P. A. R. portfolio page might look like this:

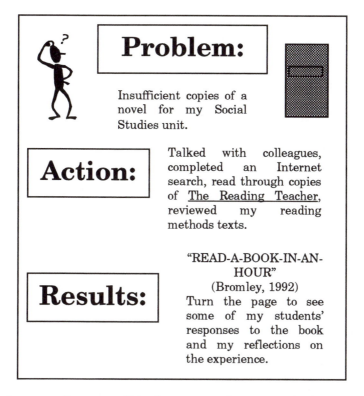

Focusing on what you *did* about something may help you select artifacts and write reflections that better communicate your abilities.

While these steps are helpful if you have been asked to submit a portfolio for a particular position, what should you do if a portfolio is not required? Is there any reason to go to the work to collect and reflect on a number of artifacts when there's already so much to do every day?

According to the professional literature, the answer is a definite yes (Jacobson, 1997). As Glatthorn (1996) notes: "Implementing a portfolio will be worth your effort even if it does nothing more than help you consistently focus on explaining to your students why they are being asked to learn the material you teach in your classroom" (p. 4).

Another reason to create a professional portfolio (whether or not you ever submit it to someone) is to augment your own professional growth. Developing a portfolio requires a different kind of thinking than many professional activities. Thinking about what it means to be a teacher and how we carry out that role helps each of us become more aware of our personal strengths and accomplishments—and thus better able to share them with others.

We also become more aware of areas we'd like to address—and often as we seek further information on a given topic, we see ways to improve our practice. As we consider how our experiences mesh with the expectations and desires of others (as in comparing job descriptions with our actual performance) we can see areas of potential reward and set goals to meet challenges (Cook, 1997).

Along these lines, you may decide to create a professional portfolio not to attain a specific teaching position or advancement, but with a larger view—say to compare your experiences with the description of excellent teaching presented in the National Standards for Voluntary Teacher Certification (National Board for Professional Teaching Standards), or those of various educational accreditation agencies (e.g., NCATE).

Teacher Thoughts

I am all for portfolios. I did not...prepare one while I was student teaching or getting my credential...two years ago a friend of mine showed me hers...I was so impressed and she said it saved her during many interviews when she was tongue-tied or could not think of the "right" answers, she would show an example of [their] work, or student work—pictures which related to the question, in her portfolio. I decided to put one together myself after that. It was a lot of work...My portfolio, I think, got me my job last year...they were impressed and kept it with them to look at. Last month, the woman who interviewed me looked at my portfolio, and it definitely was in my favor!

—5th Grade Teacher,
April 1998

See page 31 to learn more about the National Board for Professional Teaching Standards, page 28 for a list of the INTASC standards, and page 29 for information about NCATE.

In creating a portfolio with an organizing rubric (such as these standards) you will discover much you have internalized about teaching—as well as areas you'd like to examine further.

Teacher Thoughts
I started a professional portfolio as part of an evaluation at work. I was not too thrilled when I began, but I have found it to be useful. If anything, it shows me that I've done more (training, education, workshops) than I realize, and I feel proud about it. I'm not planning on switching schools or districts at this point, but if I ever do, I have a great start for interviews, etc. —9th Grade Teacher, April 1998

HOW SHOULD PROFESSIONAL PORTFOLIOS BE EVALUATED?

...what is to be evaluated is guided by <u>why</u> the evaluation is being done and <u>how</u> the results are going to be used.

—Mullins, 1994 in Cook, 1997

The individual nature of portfolios can make them difficult to evaluate. If you increase validity by allowing high submitter input, you decrease reliability of the measure across candidates. If you become more selective about what submitters include in a portfolio (high administrative control), you gain more reliable scores, but may decrease validity (MacGinitie, 1993). Further, what one evaluator finds compelling may be viewed as less important by another.

To read about the power balances between portfolio submitters and the individuals or groups requiring the submission, go to page 22.

Over time, individuals and groups using portfolios try to balance these tensions by adopting a set of guidelines for creating portfolios and designing some sort of rubric to determine how well a particular submission demonstrates particular concepts. The clarity of an evaluation rubric often depends upon how explicit portfolio guidelines are, as well as how much experience evaluators have had in working with portfolios.

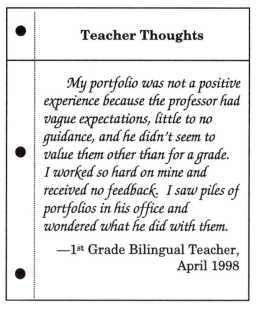

Teacher Thoughts

My portfolio was not a positive experience because the professor had vague expectations, little to no guidance, and he didn't seem to value them other than for a grade. I worked so hard on mine and received no feedback. I saw piles of portfolios in his office and wondered what he did with them.

—1st Grade Bilingual Teacher,
April 1998

46

EVALUATING PROFESSIONAL PORTFOLIOS AT THE PRESERVICE LEVEL

The nature of portfolio evaluation depends upon the purpose(s) and submitter(s) involved. Many preservice students may be asked to create professional portfolios for a single course or across courses—to document their progress in the program, and to prepare them for future professional portfolio work. This process can be overwhelming, especially for students with little or no portfolio experience.

To help alleviate student anxiety, Wagner, Brock, and Agnew (1994) suggest holding two interim portfolio reviews with college students when they are creating course portfolios. Allowing students to confer about their portfolios prior to instructor evaluation decreases anxiety and increases portfolio quality. Wagner, et al. (1994) also suggest listing important focus concepts to guide peer conferences for the best use of time. Along the same lines, Ford (1996) suggests that portfolio submitters (in this case graduate students) benefit from brainstorming criteria and then evaluating their own submissions accordingly.

Regardless of the clarity of portfolio submission and evaluation guidelines, the experience is likely to affect individuals in highly diverse ways. For example, Barton and Collins (1997) found that about half of their graduate students quickly became engaged in making sense of the portfolio experience, while the other half remained unengaged or were somewhat engaged (feeling frustrated and overwhelmed). The authors concluded that portfolio assessment is more effective if students have frequent opportunities to talk and write about their reactions to portfolios, if teachers help students make connections between coursework and portfolios, and if adequate time is scheduled for portfolio completion. If you have been asked to develop a course or program portfolio, take advantage of every opportunity to share with your peers, offer ideas for evaluation criteria, and revise your own work regularly.

EVALUATING PROFESSIONAL PORTFOLIOS AT THE INSERVICE LEVEL

While university instructors often solicit input from their students regarding portfolio submission, this is less common when inservice teachers prepare professional portfolios. If professional portfolios are new to your area, evaluation criteria may not be finalized. If you have the opportunity to help define evaluation procedures and criteria, you'll probably benefit from the experience. Whether you are able to contribute to criteria-setting or not, you may want to consider the following suggestions about evaluation to help you build a vision of what fair evaluation of your portfolio should look like.

In its guidelines for personnel evaluation, The American Evaluation Association (AEA) suggests that appropriate evaluation procedures address four categories: propriety, utility, feasibility, and accuracy (Ramlow, 1998).

Propriety. A standard of propriety requires that an evaluation be conducted "legally, ethically, and with due regard for the welfare of the evaluatees and clients of the evaluations" (p. 1). You should feel comfortable with the underlying legality and ethics of your portfolio experience. If you do not, be sure to discuss your concerns with a portfolio administrator or other professional who can address your needs.

Utility. A standard of **utility** should guide evaluation procedures so that they are informative, timely, and influential. In other words, the benefit of the evaluation should be commensurate with the effort and expense. While we can learn great deal from the process of collecting and selecting artifacts representative of various skills and abilities, we can grow even more through constructive evaluation of our work. To meet a standard of utility, you should receive feedback on your portfolio submission in a timely and useful fashion.

Otherwise, like the high school teacher's work, our professional portfolios may end up in a "filing cabinet

Teacher Thoughts
I have only used or made a portfolio twice. The first was in a teaching writing class. We had several lesson plans to incorporate, some of our writing, and ideas/lesson plans of other students in the class. This was both good and bad. It was a lot of work and a lot of stress, but I got a chance to review some things I might never have looked at again. It's in my filing cabinet somewhere.
—High School Teacher, April 1998

somewhere" if their purposes are unclear or if too much time passes between submission and feedback. If they are not clearly stated, you may want to ask about evaluation and feedback procedures when you're submitting a professional portfolio.

On a larger scale, portfolio evaluators can gain insight into the strengths and weaknesses of a particular program or approach as they peruse submissions across a number of candidates or locations. However, this insight is wasted without provisions for sharing insights and setting future goals based on the information.

Feasibility. AEA's third standard of **feasibility** calls for "evaluation systems that are as easy to implement as possible, efficient in their use of time and resources, adequately funded, and viable from a number of other standpoints" (Ramlow, 1998, p. 2). Because portfolio creation and evaluation can be expensive and time-consuming, it is important to weigh the advantages of portfolio submission carefully. You can provide important input for streamlining and improving portfolio submission procedures in your area by sharing your experiences with appropriate administrators.

Accuracy. Finally, the AEA recommends a standard of **accuracy**, requiring that assessment information be technically accurate and that conclusions be linked logically to the data. Accuracy requires that the role and responsibilities of a portfolio submitter be clearly defined. Defining what it is that submitters should know adds clarity not only to the portfolio evaluation process, but to the larger enterprise of professional development.

A GENERAL EVALUATION GUIDE

Whether you are creating a portfolio for someone else, or requiring a portfolio submission from your own students, it can be helpful to create a general evaluation rubric if one has not been provided for you. Thinking through evaluation criteria clarifies the goals and purposes of the portfolio process, and thus informs your efforts.

One way to create a rubric is to list major submission criteria in the left-hand margin of a chart (see Figure 3) and include a point scale across the top. If you have been asked to submit a portfolio with only general guidelines, you may want to use as your criteria the five general portfolio areas delineated by McLaughlin & Vogt (1996) and consider also general appearance, organization, originality, and reflection quality. You can also replace those five areas with specific standards (such as INTASC or NBPTS).

Score your portfolio as if you were an evaluator (or invite a colleague to respond to your portfolio). As you review your portfolio, you'll probably find yourself carefully defining each rubric term—and maybe even seeking a range of example entries (from ineffective to compelling). The insights you gain from these experiences will help you improve your own work prior to final submission, and will also enhance your evaluation skills for reviewing the work of others.

Standard Evaluated	Point Values			
	1 Ineffective Detracts from overall presentation	2 Marginal Does not greatly add or detract	3 Effective Helps communi-cate message	4 Compelling Enhances information presented
Title Page or Introduction				
Theme (Organization)				
Educational Philosophy				
Professional Development since Certification				
Define and Address Curriculum and Instruction				
Encourage and Document Student Growth				
Non-teaching Contributions to School and Community				
General Appearance				
Organization				
Originality				
Reflection Quality				

Figure 3 Sample evaluation rubric for a professional portfolio.

HOW CAN I IMPROVE WHAT I ALREADY DO WITH PORTFOLIOS?

Learning to teach is a life-long pursuit.

—Glatthorn, 1996

If you have completed professional portfolios in the past, you may wonder how you can improve or enhance the portfolio experience in your setting. This chapter will address five ways to improve or refocus your current portfolio efforts.

1. CREATE AN ANNUAL PORTFOLIO OF GOALS AND HOPES

One way to refocus your portfolio efforts is to create an annual portfolio. Glatthorn (1996) suggests that two weeks into the instructional year you list goals and hopes for the year. Then, at one-month intervals, review your goals and hopes and consider your progress toward them. Gather artifacts that relate to your thinking, and make notes about your selections. At the end of the year, write another reflection summarizing the progress/gains you see. Some teachers enhance this process by scheduling monthly portfolio review meetings where they share their thoughts with colleagues.

Teacher Thoughts
[In our portfolios] we included a student paper with our written feedback in letter form. ...to me, the letter to a student based on his/her paper was the most interesting and useful... We had to grade the papers and write back to the [ESL] stu-dents, addressing both higher and lower order concerns. Our [methods] teacher gave us feed-back on these letters, as did our peers. I didn't agree with every-thing she and my peers said, but it was really interesting to get feedback on something you do every day (often without thinking about it) and see how other people give feedback.   —Junior College Instructor, April 1998

2. FOCUS ON SPECIFIC SKILL DEVELOPMENT

If you want to be even more specific in your portfolio use, create a professional development portfolio focused on a particular teaching skill (Glatthorn, 1996). Select a teaching skill you'd like to refine, or one you'd like to add to your teaching repertoire. Study the concept by reading professional publications, attending conferences, speaking with colleagues, and reflecting on your ideas in writing.

Arrange to observe skilled experts. As you master the theory behind the skill, apply it in your own setting. When you're comfortable, invite a colleague to observe you. Ask him or her to provide specific feedback, rather than just general comments.

Your portfolio in this case would include notes from your study of the professional literature and conferences, feedback from colleagues, and your reflections over time. You could include samples of student work completed before, during, and after your implementation of the skill. If you share the portfolio with others, you may want to include a brief written reflection about how your teaching changed over time and how you feel about those changes.

3. REVISIT FORMAT AND FOCUS

You can also enhance your portfolio experiences by reviewing an existing portfolio you have created. How clearly does it address its purpose and audience? Is there an organizing theme that links the contents? Are all the artifacts necessary? Do they enhance one another? Are there reflections or items with unclear links to the portfolio theme? Did you consider how the portfolio was to be evaluated and clearly address required criteria? What will happen to your next portfolio upon its completion?

You may find it helpful to revise a portfolio using criteria Dennis (1995) developed for her students' writing portfolios. As students select artifacts, they consider the acronym **AIR**:

- "A" entries demonstrate **ACHIEVEMENT** and excellence;
- "I" entries demonstrate **IMPROVEMENT** and progress in any area;
- "R" entries demonstrate **REFLECTION** and personal writing that "mirrors ideas and values at a particular time" (p. 484).

Students create a Table of Contents by listing the date, title of the entry, criteria code, and a justification for placing the piece in their portfolios. In like manner, you might consider how each piece in your portfolio demonstrates a particular aspect of professional growth—or whether some pieces fail to clearly connect to the overall theme of your work.

If you've been assigned a professional portfolio and are feeling some frustration, you may want to clarify guidelines, get involved in creating portfolio evaluation criteria, and/or participate in structured peer interviews prior to the final evaluation of portfolios (Allen, 1994; Roeder, 1994; Valeri-Gold, et al., 1992; Wagner, et al., 1994; Wilcox, 1996).

 You may want to review the **Portfolio Planning Guides** beginning on page 73 for ideas on refocusing, or the questions on pages 16-17.

4. Try a Collaborative Portfolio

You can extend your portfolio repertoire by experimenting with Hoffman's (1995) concept of family portfolios. Try involving your students' whole families in the portfolio process as a way to enhance home-school connections. You can invite parent and sibling response to student work, exchange personal notes with parents, encourage each family to document important family events in their student's portfolio, etc. When it's time for you to recount your experiences in connecting with the community, you can describe the collaborative work in your own professional portfolio.

You can also extend this idea to your school "family" by proposing a grade-level or school-wide collaborative portfolio. Throughout the year, faculty members and/or students work together to create a professional portfolio that reflects the growth and accomplishments of a grade level or school. Again, when you address collaboration in your personal portfolio, you can draw upon the collaborative portfolio for examples of group accomplishments and interactions.

5. GO ELECTRONIC

Many educators now communicate electronically through email and chat rooms, and you can join conversations there about professional portfolios—and almost anything else! If you're not familiar with the Internet, this is an excellent area in which to focus your professional development efforts.

 If you feel overwhelmed by the terminology associated with electronic communications, you may want to begin your journey by reading the article by Lapp, Flood, and Lundgren (1995), referenced on page 93.

If you haven't tried them already, electronic formats provide an interesting new twist for both professional and student portfolio development. You may want to peruse some of the educational software available to help create electronic portfolios, or surf the Internet for ideas.

 To read more about electronic portfolios, go to page 63. A reference list of websites and portfolio software begins on page 88.

WHAT SHOULD I KNOW ABOUT ELECTRONIC PORTFOLIOS?

With an electronic portfolio, information can be stored digitally on a computer hard drive or some sort of removable media...this electronic information takes up very little physical space and is easily accessed. No more hunting through piles to find what you are looking for!

—Worchester, 1998

During the past decade, portfolios have been adapted from their use in elementary and secondary writing classrooms to enhance assessment and reflection on college campuses, support faculty development, and address other issues. One of the latest developments in portfolio use involves creating electronic portfolios. Just like paper-based portfolios, electronic portfolios are finding homes in almost every conceivable place—and for a myriad of purposes.

Guhlin (1996) defines electronic portfolios as "concise, annotated collections of student work that reflect educational standards" (p. 2). Like paper-based portfolios, electronic portfolios are records of student learning, growth, and change. The annotations ideally focus on student ownership and reflection, and the contents are selected to document students' abilities and understandings.

One of the most obvious advantages of electronic portfolios over their paper-based progenitors is the ease of storage and transportability, since one CD-ROM disk can hold the equivalent of 300,000 typed text pages (Lankes, 1995). Another advantage is that portfolios can be created according to a teacher-made (or professionally purchased) template.

Using a basic template for portfolios provides for some standardization in format and content across a particular group, while still allowing portfolio creators a wide berth for creativity and individual expression. You can include scanned or digital photos, video and sound clips, animations, text, traditional writings and drawings—all on the same screen or accessible with hypertext links (Guhlin, 1996). Electronic portfolios are also easy to upgrade and reorganize, and their contents can be cross-referenced in any number of ways.

While a video or cassette tape can be included with a paper-based portfolio to augment its contents, viewers or evaluators must remove a tape, insert it into a machine, cue it, review it, and replace it in the correct portfolio container. In contrast, electronic portfolios can include video and audio clips accompanied by text or graphics, all accessed at the click of a mouse. For example, an electronic portfolio might include video footage and/or audio recordings of a teacher reading aloud to students or interacting with a small group. Imagine the opportunities for viewers to "get to know" a portfolio author and his or her teaching context through multimedia links!

On the downside, electronic portfolios require some fairly sophisticated computer equipment and software, as well as the knowledge and skill to use these tools. Even in cases where such materials are available, learning to manipulate both hardware and software to create a multimedia portfolio can be a daunting process. However, like the payoffs inherent in creating paper portfolios, you'll win two ways from working with electronic portfolios. First, you'll learn a great deal about electronic communications and how these developments can support your teaching. Second, you'll able to share your knowledge with your students and help them better utilize technology for their own purposes (Worchester, 1998).

 Some websites with example electronic portfolios created by students are referenced on page 89. A list of some commercial and no-cost sources to help you create an electronic portfolio appears on page 88.

Another challenge in creating electronic portfolios is the unreliability or inaccessibility of some software and hardware. Internet access is limited in some settings, and, depending upon your computer capabilities, the actual time it takes to connect to a site can be extensive. It is also frustrating to access a site and encounter malfunctioning, incomplete, or outdated links. Further, downloading information from interesting sites to your own computer can require large amounts of memory (as well as time).

Although frustrating, problems like these need not prove fatal to your electronic portfolio efforts! Challenges can be addressed as you gain facility with the Internet, discover harmonious software and hardware configurations, and/or locate an experienced "net mentor" for advice! If you enter the world of electronic portfolio-building willing to learn *patiently*, you'll probably find much to enjoy.

Two cautions are important if you are considering electronic portfolios. First, both you and your students must be vigilant and evaluate the credibility of web sites, since almost anything can be found therein. Second, remember that others can access your websites—so don't include anything you wouldn't want copied or adapted unless you take appropriate steps to protect it. Because issues of Internet copyright are still hazy, exercise caution regarding items you both copy from or include in various websites.

Evaluating Electronic Portfolios

Electronic portfolios can be evaluated like more traditional portfolios, or you can apply additional scoring criteria related to the creator's use of media (in the case where individuals are expected to create electronic portfolios on their own). This scoring may be explicit, with accompanying rubrics, or more implicit, as in the effect on a viewer who accesses a job candidate's electronic portfolio.

To score an electronic portfolio from a technical perspective, you may want to create a rubric like the one in Figure 4. List specific requirements in the leftmost column and select point values to appear across the top. As with traditional portfolios, evaluation should involve the portfolio submitter and the evaluator(s) in a continual feedback loop.

Standard Evaluated	Point Values			
	1 Ineffective Detracts from overall presentation	2 Marginal Does not greatly add or detract	3 Effective Helps communicate message	4 Compelling Enhances information presented
Title Page or Introduction				
Theme (Organization)				
Buttons or Links (Navigability)				
Video/Audio Selections				

Figure 4 Sample scoring rubric for electronic portfolios.

WHAT ARE THE PROS AND CONS IN USING PROFESSIONAL PORTFOLIOS?

Portfolios are a means, not an end.

—Wolf & Siu-Runyan, 1996

Because professional portfolios address some instructional and assessment needs in unique and pleasing ways, it is tempting to attribute an almost magical quality to them. Surely an innovation that encourages personal ownership and learning is something to shout about! And yet, even as we celebrate all that is good about professional portfolios—and look forward to all that we may discover about their use in the future—it is important to exercise wisdom and caution in our expectations. A brief consideration of some benefits and shortcomings of professional portfolios can help us maintain a balanced perspective.

Some Benefits Associated with Professional Portfolios

In a sense, we can list the benefits of professional portfolios next to each use. For example, if you create a professional portfolio to keep track of your personal growth and learning over a period of time, you gain the benefit of systematic reflection. If you draw upon a set of standards (e.g., INTASC, NBPTS) to organize your portfolio, you discover strengths in your approaches and new ways to think about your professional efforts. In a world filled with numerous demands on our time, creating a portfolio invites us to slow down, rethink, rehearse, and reflect. Is it possible to do those things without creating a professional portfolio? Of course! But the question is, do we?

The benefits of creating a professional portfolio can extend beyond our own development to that of our students. By creating your own portfolio, you become familiar with the ins and the outs of the process. If you've struggled over what an artifact represents, labored to express your feelings about an experience, wondered deeply about an issue—imagine the shared community you can build with and for the children in your classroom as they do the same. Your ability to empathize will help you predict problem areas and provide support where it is most likely to be needed (Murnane, 1994).

Engaging in the portfolio process can also encourage and enhance relationships among peers and colleagues. While it's not likely that you'll suddenly relate with *everyone*, if you take advantage of the opportunity to share your portfolio experiences with colleagues and students (both the highs <u>and</u> the lows), you may discover new ways to communicate about the profession as well as about your needs and challenges within its confines. You may be surprised at the relationships that will blossom as you seek out and share with like-minded individuals. And you may be even more surprised at what transpires with those who challenge your thinking! Indeed, individuals who engage in portfolio sharing often become close mentors and friends—certainly a professional bonus! Additionally, sharing with others can help assuage fears, support our efforts to try new ideas, and stimulate pursuit of professional knowledge (McLauglin & Vogt, 1996; Stewart & Paradis, 1993 in Bergeron, et al., 1997).

Moving beyond the local setting, implementing portfolios on a large-scale basis can offer potential benefits as well. As P. Roeder notes (personal communication, April 17, 1998), using portfolios to evaluate an entire undergraduate program provides unique information about how students view and interpret their coursework. Several changes in the Liberal Studies major at San Diego State University grew out of portfolio indicators, and the same is true in many other places. When evaluators read particular subject area essays by numerous students, they can detect patterns and devise course changes to address misinterpretations or disjointed ideas.

Some Concerns Associated with Professional Portfolios

Although much enthusiasm about portfolios is warranted, it is important to remember that the greatest strengths of portfolios also contribute to their greatest weaknesses (Valencia, 1990; Wolf & Siu-Runyan, 1996). The very fact that portfolios allow for a great range of individual expression means that they can be extremely difficult to evaluate on a large-scale basis. Evaluating large numbers of portfolios generally leads to standardization—of at least some aspects. It's a "Catch-22" of sorts: Suddenly, something that was useful because of its ability to portray individuality is being standardized so it can be used more widely.

In our enthusiasm for what portfolios appear to do, we should avoid overstating their usefulness—or overextending their application. For example, because portfolios often provide information we don't always derive from more traditional measures, some people believe portfolio assessment should be widely implemented in place of standardized testing. Certainly standardized measures encompass their own pros and cons, but perhaps it makes more sense to discover how various portfolios relate to other measures before we dismiss those measures entirely.

Along these lines, another challenge inherent in using portfolios is the question of how to achieve fairness and reliability when they are reviewed. Short of complete standardization of submission and evaluation procedures, how can those using portfolios on a large-scale basis guarantee that one reviewer's assessment of a particular portfolio will be consistent with that of other reviewers—or even with the same reviewer over time?

Granted, institutions and large groups generally approach the problem of reliable review by continually updating and clarifying submission and evaluation criteria, and by supporting ongoing training and feedback for evaluation team members. While these efforts are important, there's much more to be learned in this area. As we participate in various professional portfolio experiences, we can contribute to the growing knowledge base by refining our own understanding of how and when professional portfolios work well.

Another challenge in professional portfolio implementation involves the highly selective nature of building a portfolio. How portfolio submitters are introduced to the process, as well as the guidance they receive in making artifact selections and presenting them greatly affects implementation of portfolio assessment. Although Afflerbach, Kapinus, and DeLain (1995) were speaking of student portfolio assessment, their comments may apply equally well to individuals submitting professional portfolios:

> ...no assessment or series of assessments, regardless of their validity or usefulness, can compensate for students not being exposed to information; not having the opportunity to participate in hands-on learning; or not being engaged in discussions that force them to expand, reflect upon, critically evaluate, justify, and defend their thinking. Without the appropriate support, performance-based assessment will only emphasize what's not happening in the classroom and the school.... (p. 441)

In one of the first efforts of its kind, the National Board for Professional Teaching Standards is addressing the need to support teachers as they create professional portfolios. Beginning this summer, candidates who apply for and do not receive national certification may "bank" passing evaluation scores from parts of the process. When they reapply for certification the following year, they need only address the areas that did not pass. This differentiated feedback helps teachers more clearly identify where they should focus their improvement efforts. Over time, such support policies will probably become widespread—as individuals and groups learn to tailor professional portfolio submission and evaluation to the needs in their settings. Again, there is much to be explored regarding teacher support in the portfolio process.

Additional Areas to Address in Professional Portfolio Assessment

Despite the positive developments in support for professionals engaging in the portfolio process, it is important to remember that performance-based assessment has not solved all of our assessment challenges with young children, nor will it address *every* issue related to professional certification and growth. Noting that the health fields have long relied on performance-based assessments of various types, Swanson, Norman, and Linn (1995) describe six lessons from the medical field which can be instructive for those involved in creating professional portfolios.

Judging Effectiveness. It is important to realize that just because portfolios are designed to demonstrate "realistic" performance settings doesn't mean that the evidence collected actually demonstrates teacher effectiveness. For example, what does including a program from a school musical in a professional portfolio actually represent? Even if it is accompanied by a teacher's reflective statement, does it accurately portray the teacher's skill in teaching students to sing or play instruments?

Interpreting Guidelines. Both portfolio submitters and evaluators must engage in a high degree of interpretation. Regardless of the clarity of submission or evaluation guidelines, the question of exactly what skills or competencies a particular set of criteria is designed to elicit can be difficult to answer. Further, what one person defines as a teaching competency may differ greatly from another's view.

The question of appropriate artifact selection also poses a challenge. How can a portfolio submitter be confident that his or her selection of particular artifacts actually exhibits the skill in question? While some submissions may be straightforward, such as a request for a copy of a current teaching credential, others may be almost impossible to interpret. This leads to the next area of concern, that of alternate responses.

Scoring Alternate Responses. Given the need for both submitter and evaluator to interpret guidelines, what is an evaluator to do if a portfolio submission appears to meet a criterion—but in a way so unique it's difficult to explain or rate? How many alternate responses are reasonable within or across portfolios? Is it fair to reward some unique responses and not others? In the absence of clear examples of "appropriate" submissions, what are submitters to do if they disagree with an evaluation? The question of how to handle alternate responses can and should be raised whenever professional portfolios are used.

Performing in Different Contexts. Another critical issue related to professional development involves the effect of context on someone's teaching. How many of us are comfortable and effective in one setting, but have to "start over" when we change contexts? If a teacher creates a portfolio that demonstrates effectiveness in one setting, what implications does this have for his or her performance in other locations? Swanson, et al. (1995) note that, for medical students, performance in one context does not necessarily predict performance in another. If the same is true of educators, what are the implications for professional portfolio assessment across contexts?

Comparing Portfolio Results to Other Measures. In the health fields, performance-based measurements do not relate consistently to other assessment results (Swanson, et al., 1995). This may be good news—suggesting that performance-based assessments address areas of competence not assessed by other means. On the other hand, it may suggest that performance-based assessments are highly situational and context-bound—providing little information beyond the fact that someone accomplished something in a particular setting on a specific day. Further study of the relationship between professional portfolios and actual teacher effectiveness (defined and measured in multiple ways) is needed before we can comfortably conclude that a teacher who creates a marvelous portfolio is also a marvelous teacher.

Realizing the Impact of High-Stakes Evaluation. Because professional portfolios are often used for high-stakes decisions such as certification, licensure, and promotion, it is important to investigate the effect of the assessment on teachers. Do teachers who spend a great deal of time creating a professional portfolio become better teachers? Or are they actually less effective in the classroom because they are preoccupied and concerned about creating their portfolios? Do some professionals benefit more from creating professional portfolios than others?

Those working with preservice students have suggested that portfolio creation can be overwhelming—and that students benefit from support during the process. Is this also true of professionals? What kind of support is most helpful? Questions like these should be raised consistently and investigated thoroughly as we explore professional portfolios and other performance-based assessments of teachers.

Looking Toward The Future: Choosing Our Own Adventures

Calfee and Perfumo (1993) suggest that student portfolios may contribute to real change in classrooms if their use is not short-circuited by three major challenges—challenges which may also apply to professional portfolios. These challenges occur when: 1) Professionals lack an appropriate, appreciative audience for their portfolios, 2) Over-standardization renders individual portfolios too similar, and 3) Keepers of the status quo view teacher empowerment through portfolios as a threat to traditional power structures.

The relative newness of portfolio use in education offers some hope that we can address challenges and concerns while maintaining the benefits we have seen thus far. In many places, submission and evaluation criteria for various portfolio applications are still evolving. This allows for individuals to have a voice in the direction of their schools, districts, and other institutions. It also helps avoid the "etched in stone" feeling surrounding more traditional or standardized measures. If a professional portfolio process doesn't address the needs of a particular group, it can be modified in endless ways—as long as we remain open to the possibilities of change.

The current dynamism in professional portfolio assessment mirrors the ever-changing panorama of human growth and achievement. The "choose-your-own adventure" nature of teaching and learning attracted many of us to the education enterprise. Professional portfolios offer many exciting opportunities for each of us to chart new ground by continuing to "choose our own adventures" in professional development.

SECTION TWO

PLANNING GUIDES FOR CREATING YOUR PROFESSIONAL PORTFOLIO

Academic Portfolios are created in formal academic settings to enhance course learning, achieve course credit, and demonstrate accomplishment in a specific program of study. On the next eight pages, you will find the following planning pages to help you create particular professional portfolios:

- Professional Portfolio Preplanning Guide (Selecting the correct professional portfolio to create), p. 74
- Portfolio Planner for a Working Portfolio, pp. 75-77
- Portfolio Planner for Admission to a Program of Study, pp. 78-79
- *Portfolio Planner for Certification, pp. 80-81*

Professional Advancement Portfolios are created in professional settings such as the classroom where you teach. They are intended to help you answer personal questions, meet professional challenges, and advance in your career. Planning guides for professional portfolios appear on the following pages:

- *Portfolio Planner for Professional Development (to be shared with others), pp. 82-83*
- Portfolio Planner for Action Research (for personal research growth), p. 84
- Portfolio Planner for a Custom Portfolio, p. 85

PROFESSIONAL PORTFOLIO PREPLANNING GUIDE

Consider each question in planning your portfolio.
Circle the response closest to your own or write in your ideas.

QUESTIONS	RESPONSES
• *Why am I creating a portfolio?*	To gain personal insight or improve my teaching?
	To enter an academic program?
	To advance professionally?
• *What will I include in my portfolio?*	Paper only?
	Multidimensional items (video or audiotapes, etc.)?
	How many items?
• *When will I collect and organize the samples and artifacts?*	A period of time such as a semester or grading period?
	Longer?
	Shorter?
• How will I display and present my collection?	Files?
	Binder?
	Plastic Box?
	Electronic Format?
	Other?
• Who am I as a learner and who am I sharing this portfolio with?	Am I demonstrating what I have done or what I want to do?
	Who is my major audience?
• Who might help me select or review the contents of my portfolio?	Who has done this before?
	Who has reviewed portfolios like mine?
	Who has a role similar to the one I'm seeking?
• Where is this portfolio going and how can my choices best facilitate that journey?	How can I organize this so that the contents can be easily (and correctly) replaced after review?
	How might I protect items which can break or be lost?
• What other questions do I have?	Where will I seek the answers?

The Portfolio Planner for a
WORKING PORTFOLIO

PURPOSE:
To systematically collect items for use in a future portfolio (the type as yet undetermined)—so they all will be in one place.

AUDIENCE:
You'll collect primarily for yourself at the beginning. Your audience will be defined more clearly later, when you settle on a portfolio focus.

CONTAINER:
Since this is an open-ended collection, you may want to use a large file box or plastic tub so videotapes, etc. can be collected here. Paper materials may be collected in file folders.

TIME FRAME (for materials collection):
Can extend for any amount of time—from the beginning of a semester to the end; the beginning of a school year to the end, during a program (such as throughout a teacher preparation or graduate program) etc.

SECTION 1: INTRODUCTORY MATERIALS

Artifacts/Purposes (These are only suggestions: Use your creativity here!)	Examples/Variations (List other ideas.)	Date (When filed or attained.)
• Items to introduce you (and your students) such as: resume, photo, brief written description of yourself and how you fulfill particular teaching roles, brief philosophy statement about teaching, etc.		
• Ideas/themes for your reader to navigate the eventual portfolio.		
• Possible uses for your portfolio—potential audiences or goals.		

SECTION 2: TEACHER PREPARATION EXPERIENCES

Artifacts/Purposes	Examples/Variations	Date
• Academic transcript(s), official certifications from your discipline.		
• Reports/evaluations of career-related work experiences (e.g., student teaching reports, internship).		
• Awards, honors, certificates from special training.		
• Handwriting sample (especially if you're seeking your first position and will be instructing in an elementary setting).		

SECTION 2 (Continued): TEACHER PREPARATION EXPERIENCES		
Artifacts/Purposes	**Examples/Variations**	**Date**
• Sample of your own creative and/or academic writing.		
• Pictures/videotapes that demonstrate special skills you have, clients you have worked with, projects you have done (e.g., bulletin boards, art projects).		
• Required certificates, credentials, health documents (e.g., TB test), etc.		

STOP!
Look through the materials you have collected. What do you notice about yourself and your preparation? Jot down your thoughts and include them in your file.

SECTION 3: INSERVICE TEACHING EXPERIENCES		
Artifacts/Purposes	**Examples/Variations**	**Date**
• Items you have created (e.g., teaching tools, art projects, special reports).		
• Documentation of technical or computer skills that could benefit your employer.		
• Introduction of your classroom community (rules, routines, schedules, organization of space and materials, general documentation of student learning/growth).		
• Letters of commendation or thanks from people/students you have worked with.		
• A program from an event you planned.		
• Listing of specific courses, conferences, etc. you have attended and notes about their impact on your thinking/teaching.		
• Sample of your students' work before and after a specific intervention.		
• Journal entry that exhibits your ability to reflect on your practice and/or learning.		

SECTION 3 (continued): INSERVICE TEACHING EXPERIENCES		
Artifacts/Purposes	Examples/Variations	Date
• Programs/routines you have instituted on a classroom (or larger) basis and their effect on student learning and growth.		
• Examples of how you plan or carry out a particular learning sequence.		
• Evidence of ways you support students' social development and value diversity of perspective, background, language, etc.		
• How you select, adapt, and utilize resources to address a particular need.		
• How you assess your own performance and learning, as well as that of students.		
• Evidence of work outside the classroom with families, with the profession, or other related ways.		
• Newspaper articles (or other publications) that address your achievements.		
• Evidence of collaboration with colleagues and its effects on your teaching, your school, etc.		
SECTION 4: ADDITIONAL ITEMS TO CONSIDER		
Artifacts/Purposes	Examples/Variations	Date
• Language experiences (Do you speak/read/write in other languages? To what level of proficiency?).		
• Experiences in diverse settings (multicultural, multilingual, special needs students, etc.).		
• Unique personality traits or skills especially valuable in achieving your stated goals.		
• Letters of recommendation for specific skills, contributions, experiences.		
• Documentation about achievements (e.g., how membership in a particular honor society is achieved).		

The Portfolio Planner for
ADMISSION TO A PROGRAM OF STUDY

NOTE: Read through the ideas in the WORKING PORTFOLIO Planner Pages (pp. 75-77) as well as those listed below. You may want to combine concepts from both of these worksheets for your finished product.

PURPOSE:
To showcase your educational background, skills, and experiences to gain admission to a particular program of study.

AUDIENCE:
University admissions committee members, graduate admissions officers, committees of education professors and faculty related to your discipline.

CONTAINER:
If the container is not specified in submission guidelines, consider how the portfolio will most likely be reviewed. If several people will look through it, you may want to use a three ring binder with divider pages or some other easily transported container. You may want to avoid unwieldy files and boxes filled with materials that can be easily dropped or misplaced.

TIME FRAME (for materials collection):
Usually includes recent educational and academic experiences as well as a summary of key secondary school experiences related to your goal(s).

SECTION 1: KEY HIGH SCHOOL/SECONDARY PREPARATION
(Include only this section if applying for admission to a college program)

Artifacts/Purposes (These are only suggestions: Use your creativity here!)	Examples/Variations (List other ideas.)	Date (When filed or attained.)
• Brief Resume.		
• Academic Transcript(s).		
• Extracurricular Activities (and how they relate to your current goal).		
• Sample of your academic writing (if required).		
• Employment Experiences.		
• Community Service.		
• Other requirements listed in admission materials:		
• _____	_____	_____
• _____	_____	___
• _____	_____	___
• _____	_____	___
• _____		___
• _____		
• _____		___

SECTION 2: KEY UNDERGRADUATE PREPARATION

(Include this section if applying for admission to a teacher education program after completing some college study—you may extend the categories above by adding more recent material, or address them separately. If you are applying for advanced/graduate study, extend this section to include your most recent academic achievements and limit attention devoted to secondary school experiences.)

Artifacts/Purposes	Examples/Variations	Date
• Employment Experiences (especially ways your employment has prepared you for a teaching career).		
• Community Service, (especially work with children and/or teaching experiences).		
• Other requirements listed in admission materials:		
• _____	_____	_____
• _____	_____	_____
• _____	_____	_____
• _____	_____	

SECTION 3: ADDITIONAL ITEMS TO CONSIDER

Artifacts/Purposes	Examples/Variations	Date
• Language experiences (Do you speak/read/write more than one language? To what level of proficiency?).		
• Experiences in diverse settings (multicultural, multilingual, special needs students, etc.).		
• Unique personality traits or skills especially valuable in achieving your stated goals.		
• Other?		
• _____	_____	_____
• _____	_____	_____
• _____	_____	_____
• _____	_____	_____
• _____		

71

The Portfolio Planner for a
CERTIFICATION PORTFOLIO

NOTE: Read through the ideas for the WORKING PORTFOLIO as well as those listed below. You may want to combine concepts from both of these planning guides for your finished product.

PURPOSE:
To detail your accomplishments in a specific area and/or your readiness to receive a particular proficiency designation such as graduation from a particular program or professional teaching certification.

AUDIENCE:
University evaluation committee; national, state, or local licensure board members.

CONTAINER:
Check submission guidelines. If not specified, consider the most transportable method that accommodates your selections.

TIME FRAME (for materials collection):
Can extend for any amount of time—from the beginning of a semester to the end; the beginning of a school year to the end, during a program (e.g., throughout a teacher preparation or graduate program).

SECTION 1: INTRODUCTORY MATERIALS

Artifacts/Purposes (These are only suggestions: Use your creativity here!)	Examples/Variations (List other ideas.)	Date (When filed or attained.)
• Items which introduce you such as: resume, photo, brief written description of yourself and how you fulfill particular teaching roles, brief philosophy statement about teaching.		
• Ideas/themes for your reader to navigate the portfolio.		
• Other ideas?		

SECTION 2: KEY REQUIREMENTS FOR GRADUATION/CERTIFICATION

Artifacts/Purposes (List each major requirement for graduation or certification.)	Examples/Variations (List how you will document each requirement.)	Date (When filed or attained.)
•		
•		
•		
•		
•		
•		

SECTION 3: OTHER RELATED ACHIEVEMENTS TO HIGHLIGHT		
Artifacts/Purposes (List other achievements to include.)	**Examples/Variations** (List how you will document each achievement.)	**Date** (When filed or attained.)
•		
•		
•		
•		
•		
•		
•		
•		
•		
•		
•		
•		
•		
•		
•		
•		
•		
•		
•		
•		
•		
•		
•		
•		
•		
•		
•		
•		
•		
•		
•		
•		
•		
•		
•		
•		
•		

PROFESSIONAL DEVELOPMENT PORTFOLIO

PURPOSE:
To document the genesis, development, and result(s) of a professional growth activity. This usually centers on a professional development goal, such as career advancement.

AUDIENCE:
Could include: professional evaluation committee, building administrator, district administrators, peers.

CONTAINER:
May be specified in guidelines. If not, probably a three-ring binder with representative problem-action-results documentation will be best.

TIME FRAME (for materials collection):
Can extend for any amount of time—from the beginning of a marking period to the end; the beginning of a school year to the end, over a period of probationary tenure, etc.

SECTION 1: INTRODUCTORY MATERIALS

Artifacts/Purposes (These are only suggestions: Use your creativity here!)	Examples/Variations (List other ideas.)	Date (When filed or attained.)
• Ideas/themes to navigate the portfolio.		
• Possible uses for your portfolio—other potential audiences or goals?		

SECTION 2: SUMMARY OF THE QUESTION OR CHALLENGE

Artifacts/ Purposes	Examples/Variations	Date
• What was the question or challenge which led to your project choice?		
• What was the extent of the question/challenge and its effects in your professional development (e.g., was a student behavior problem disrupting class learning and your professional satisfaction?).		

SECTION 3: SUMMARY OF ACTIONS TAKEN		
Artifacts/ Purposes	**Examples/Variations**	**Date**
• Chronological summary of actions taken.		
• Representative samples of action taken (e.g., program from a related professional workshop, transcript from an extended study course, photocopy of an influential research article). • _____ • _____ • _____ • _____	_____ _____	_____ _____
• Excerpts from personal reflective journal documenting your growth and insights.		
SECTION 4: SUMMARY OF RESULTS AND FUTURE GOALS/DIRECTIONS		
Artifacts/Purposes	**Examples/Variations**	**Date**
• Results of each action. • _____ • _____ • _____ • _____	_____ _____	_____ _____
• Future goals/research resulting from current effort (e.g., list of professional courses you'll take, new research questions arising out of former one, inservice sessions you'll present).		

The Portfolio Planner for
ACTION RESEARCH

PURPOSE:
To detail your thoughts and actions related to a professional development goal and/or action research project.

AUDIENCE:
Yourself.

CONTAINER:
Since this is an open-ended collection, you may want to use a large file box or plastic tub so videotapes, etc. can be collected here. Paper materials may be collected in file folders.

TIME FRAME (for materials collection):
Usually covers at least one marking period, but can extend to a semester, academic year, or beyond. Be sure and set a regular time to make entries on this page.

Problem or Question: Musings and Notes		Action to be Taken (or Action Taken)	Result(s)
(Use this format to note questions or concerns, ongoing thoughts or insights. It will serve as a reflective journal from which you can select important insights if you later decide to share your development with others.)		(List other ideas that occur to you as you go along so they won't be forgotten.)	(Expected or actual—you may also want to include a description of artifacts that document this problem-action-result sequence and where they can be found in your container.)
Date	Ideas/What I Wonder		

The Portfolio Planner for

_____

This page will help you plan your own portfolio. Review the other guides for ideas and then complete this one.

PURPOSE:
AUDIENCE:
CONTAINER:
TIME FRAME (for materials collection):

Possible Time Table and Areas of Focus (Fill in dates to achieve particular goals as well as areas you wish to address.)	Possible Artifacts (List artifacts that may demonstrate particular accomplishments and achieve-ments?)	Variations and Notes (List other ideas that occur to you so they won't be forgotten.)	How & When Accomplished (How and when will you achieve this?)

You may not be able to tell, but this is a rain forest "tree" we created in our classroom this year. The rain forest is one of my favorite things to teach. I've been to rain forests twice—and during both experiences I was so moved by the beauty!

When I teach this unit I bring tons of photos from my trips and share personal experiences with the students. They are fascinated with everything I share and they have so many great questions! During our unit, we read great books about the rain forest, and the children make the animals you see on the tree and near it.

I think it would be helpful to include pictures like this in a professional portfolio to help me explain the environment I create in my classroom.

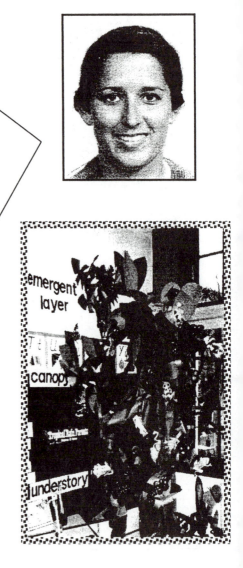

SECTION THREE

REFERENCES FOR OTHER
PROFESSIONAL PORTFOLIO JOURNEYS

PROFESSIONAL/COMMERCIAL SOURCES FOR ELECTRONIC PORTFOLIO DEVELOPMENT

Sample Software and Commercial Sites

- **Claris FileMaker Pro**: Software for creating electronic portfolios.
  Brewer, G. (1994). Santa Clara, CA: Claris Corporation.
- **Claris Home Page**: Software for creating electronic portfolios.
  www.claris.com/products/claris/clarispage/claris
- **Grady Profile**: Template for teachers and students.
  Grady, M. P. (1991). St. Louis, MO: Aurbach & Associates, Inc.
- **HyperStudio**: Software for creating electronic portfolios.
  http://www.hsj.com/hsj.html
  Wagner, R. (1993). El Cajon, CA: Roger Wagner Publishing, Inc.
- **Influxx**: Help with online resume and portfolios.
  http://www.influxx.com/pricing.htm
- **PersonaPlus**: Multimedia student and teacher portfolios, assessment, curriculum resource management.
  http://WWW.PersonaPlus.COM/

Representative College & University Sites

- **Griffith University**:
  http://www.gu.edu.au/gwis/gihe/tp_home.html
- **Ohio University**: Step by step instructions and downloadable templates for creating electronic student portfolios. While designed for students in business majors, much is applicable across disciplines.
  http://sirius.cba.ohiou.edu/~mgt300/ESP/portfolio.htm
- **St. Norbert College**:
  http://www.snc.edu/educ/edpages/portfolio.html
- **University of Virginia/Curry School of Education**: Course syllabus for class where electronic teaching portfolios are created with INTASC standards as the framework.
  http://curry.edschool.virginia.edu/curry/class/edes/589_004/description.html
- **Wayne State University**: Although geared toward college professors, links on this website provide ideas that can be adapted to other settings.
  http://www.lib.wayne.edu/otl/portfol.html

- **Wichita State University**:
  http://www.twsu.edu/~coewww/portfolio2.html
  http://www.cua.edu/www/eric_ae/Infoguide/port_he.txt
- **University of Florida**:
  http://www.unf.edu/~tbratina/cdrom.htm

General Websites

- **Creating a homepage**:
  http://members.aol.com/teachemath/create.htm
- **Electronic portfolio scoring rubric**:
  http://www.essdack.org.port/rubric.htlm
- **Html homepage flowchart**:
  http://members.aol.com/teachemath/flowch1.htm
- **HTML made really easy**: http://www.jmarshall.com/easy/html
- **Learning to create web pages and navigate the web**:
  http://www.ncsa.uiuc.edu/General/Internet/WWW/HTMLPrimerA
  ll.html
- **Making active links, Free beginning web page**:
  http:www.geocities.com/SiliconValley/Campus/1924/link.html
- **Top 15 mistakes of first time web design**:
  wysiwyg://659/http://www.doghause.com/top15.html

Examples of Electronic Portfolios Created by Students

- http://www.sv400.k12.ks.us/port/example1.html
- http://www.sv400.k12.ks.us/port/example2.html
- http://www2.ncsu.edu/ncsu/cep.ligon/passports.html

EDUCATION ORGANIZATIONS AND WEBSITES

Organizations that Address Educational Issues and Standards

- **American Association of Colleges for Teacher Education**
  (AACTE) http://www.aacte.org
- **American Association of Higher Education** (AAHE)
- **American Federation of Teachers** (AFT)
- **Association for Supervision and Curriculum Development**
  (ASCD) http://www.ascd.org/
- **Association of Teacher Educators** (ATE)
- **Carnegie Foundation for the Advancement of Teaching**
- **Center for Education Renewal**

- **International Reading Association** (IRA)
- **Interstate New Teacher Assessment and Support Consortium** (INTASC, a project of the Council of Chief State School Officers)
- **National Board for Professional Teaching Standards** (NBPTS) http://www.nbpts.org
- **National Center for Innovation**
- **National Center for Research on Teacher Learning** (NCRTL) http://www.ncrtl.msu.edu
- **National Center for Restructuring Education, Schools, and Teaching** (NCREST) http://www.tc.columbia.edu/~ncrest/
- **National Commission on Teaching and America's Future** http://www.tc.columbia.edu/~teachcomm/
- **National Council for Accreditation of Teacher Education http://www.ncate.org**
- **National Council of Teachers of English** (NCTE)
- **National Education Association** (NEA) http://www.nea.org
- **National Reading Conference** (NRC)
- **National Staff Development Council** (NSDC) http://www.nsdc.org/
- **National Teacher Policy Institute** (NTPI) http://www.teachnet.org/ntpi/
- **Teach for America**
  - **(Outside of the United States)**
- **Standards Council of the Teaching Profession** (SCTP) http://www.sofweb.vic.edu.au/standco/index.htm

Miscellaneous Materials

- **Commercial Materials:**
  http://www.neatschoolhouse.org/Office/Teacher/Assessment_Information/Portfolios.html
  http://www.tlsecrets.com/products/prod.htm
- **On-line Bookstores or Book Reviews/Ads:**
  http://www.amazon.com/
  http://206.43.189.116/library/portfolio.htm
  http://www.ascd.org/pubs/new/books/0829702book.html
  http://www.business1.com/iri_Sky/profport/ppcc.htm
- **Uses of Portfolios:**
  http://www.humankinetics.com/product/proddesc/bme10809.htm
  http://www.cua.edu.www/eric_ae/Infoguide/port_he

PORTFOLIO GLOSSARY

Accountability Portfolio	Student work, teacher records, and standardized assessments submitted according to structured guidelines. (Wolf & Siu-Runyan, 1996)
Admission Portfolio	Portfolio designed to demonstrate a student's preparedness to enter a particular program (e.g., teacher preparation), or to document a student's achievement within a program (e.g., preparedness to graduate with an undergraduate or graduate degree). Some universities are experimenting with program portfolios in lieu of more traditional senior papers, master's theses, and doctoral dissertations (cf. Palmer, Holahan, & Johnstone, 1996; Roeder, 1994).
Assessment Portfolio	Presents educational organization with information about a teacher's effectiveness. (Wolf & Dietz in Ross, 1997)
Developmental or "Ownership" Portfolio	Personalized collection of work to illustrate progress. Reflection on development of work and learning encourages personal goal-setting. May be shared with others, but is designed primarily for the owner. (Lankes, 1995; Wolf & Siu-Runyan, 1996)
Educational Portfolio	A purposeful or selective collection of student papers and projects which also includes student reflections and teacher evaluations designed to show educational progress in a particular area over a designated time. (Lankes, 1995; Wolf & Siu-Runyan, 1996)
Electronic Portfolio	Concise, annotated collections of student work that reflect educational standards created in an electronic format. (Guhlin, 1998)
Employment Portfolio	Collection of artifacts designed to show submitter's work readiness skills for prospective employers. (Lankes, 1995; Ross, 1997)
Learning Portfolio	Promotes teacher reflection and ownership over the learning process. (Wolf & Dietz in Ross, 1997)
Proficiency Portfolio	Collection of artifacts which demonstrated student competence and performance in a discipline or particular area. (Lankes, 1995; Wilcox, 1997)
Showcase Portfolio	Collection of teacher's best work during an entire educational career (or other period of time) which demonstrates specific skills and abilities. (Lankes, 1995; Wilcox, 1997)
Teacher Portfolio	Collection of work produced by a teacher . . . designed to highlight and demonstrate knowledge and skills in teaching. Also provides the means for reflection; offers the opportunity to critique one's work and evaluate the effectiveness of lessons or interpersonal interactions with students or peers. (Doolittle, 1994)
Working or Collection Portfolio	Collection of artifacts related to teaching from which you will draw a smaller, more focused collection for more extended reflection and portfolio development. Functions much like a "writer's folder" where authors collect all drafts of all of their work. (Wilcox, 1997)

REFERENCES

Afflerbach, P., Kapinus, B., & DeLain, M. T. (1995). Equity and performance-based assessment: An insider's view. The Reading Teacher, 48, 5, 440-42.

Allen, D. (1994). Portfolios: The unknown, the struggle and the learning. In S. O. Smyser, (Ed.), Encouraging reflection through portfolios (pp. 21-33). Proceedings of the National Conference on Linking Liberal Arts and Teacher Education. San Diego, CA. Sponsored by Rockefeller Brothers and University of Redlands.

Allen, D. D. (1996). Involving graduate students in personal literacy evaluation through the use of portfolios. In M. D. Collins and B. G. Moss, (Eds.), Literacy assessment for today's schools (pp. 75-81). Monograph of the College Reading Association.

Anderson, D. (1997, April 21). Same song, second verse. [On-line]. Available: http://www.aacte.org/about/presb421.html#guidelines

Barton, J. & Collins, A. (1997). Portfolio assessment: A handbook for educators. Menlo Park, CA: Addison-Wesley Publishing Company.

Bergeron, B. S., Wermuth, S., & Hammar, R. C. (1997). Initiating portfolios through shared learning: Three perspectives. The Reading Teacher, 50, 7, 552-62.

Bradley, A. (1997a, March 26). Standards board touted for elevating teaching profession. Education Week on the Web. [On-line]. Available: http://www.edweek.org/ew/vol-16/26ind.h16

Bradley, A. (1997b, September 17). NCATE told to emphasize technology. Education Week on the Web. [On-line]. Available: http://www.edweek.org/ew/vol-17/03ncate.h17

Bradley, A. (1997c, October 29). Accreditors shift toward performance. Education Week on the Web. [On-line]. Available: http://www.edweek.org/ew/vol-17/09ncate.h17

Bromley, K. D. (1992). Language arts: Exploring connections (2nd ed.). Boston: Allyn & Bacon.

Burke, K. (1996). Portfolios—A proven plan for professionals. [On-line]. Available: http://www.iriskylight.com/TrainCo2/portfo.htm

Calfee, R. C., & Perfumo, P. (1993). Student portfolios: Opportunities for a revolution in assessment. Journal of Reading, 36, 7, 532-37.

Campbell, D. M., Cignetti, P. B., Melenyzer, B. J., Nettles, D. H., & Wyman, R. M., Jr. (1997). How to develop a professional portfolio. Boston: Allyn & Bacon.

Cook, C. (1996). Critical issue: Realizing new learning for all students through professional development. [On-line]. Available: http://www.ncrel.org/sdrs/areas/issues/educatrs/profdevl/pd200.htm

Cook, C. (1997). Critical issue: Evaluating professional growth and development. [On-line]. Available: http://www.ncrel.org/sdrs/areas/issues/educatrs/profdevl/pd500.htm

Cooper, J. M. (1997, September 3). Tenure and teaching portfolios. Education Week on the Web. [On-line]. Available: http://www.edweek.org/ew/vol-17/01cooper.h17

Dennis, S. (1995). AIR is for portfolio pride. Journal of Reading, 38, 6, 484-85.

Diez, M. E. (1994). The portfolio: Sonnet, mirror and map. In S. O. Smyser, (Ed.), Encouraging reflection through portfolios (pp. 7-20). Proceedings of the National Conference on Linking Liberal Arts and Teacher Education. San Diego, CA. Sponsored by Rockefeller Brothers and University of Redlands.

Doolittle, P. (1994). Teacher portfolio assessment. ERIC/AE Digest. [On-line]. Available: http://www.ed.gov/databases/ERIC_Digests/ed385608.html

Ford, M. P. (1996). Teachers as learners: Experiencing self-evaluation, portfolios, and rubrics. In M. D. Collins & B. G. Moss, (Eds.), Literacy assessment for today's schools (pp. 82-94). Monograph of the College Reading Association.

Glatthorn, A. A. (1996). The teacher's portfolio: Fostering and documenting professional development. Rockport, MA: ProActive Publications.

Goodwin, J. P. & Hensley, R. P. (1997, 7 May). Ball State Career Services: Professional employment portfolios. [On-line]. Available: http://www.bsu.edu/careers/foliotip.html

Guhlin, M. (1996, November 20). Electronic portfolios. [On-line]. Available: http://www.esc20.k12.tx.82/techserv/materials/ppts/portfolios/sld002.htm

Haertel, E. (1990). From expert opinions to reliable scores: Psychometrics for judgment-based teacher assessment. Paper presented at the Annual Meeting of the American Educational Research Association, Boston, MA.

Hoffman, J. L. (1995). The family portfolio: Using authentic literacy assessment in family history programs. The Reading Teacher, 48, 7, 594-97.

Jacobson, L. (1997, March 5). Portfolios playing increasing role in teacher hiring, study finds. [On-line]. Education Week on the Web. Available: http://www.edweek.org/ew/vol-16/23port.h16

Johnson, D. (1997, February 15). National Commission on Teaching and America's Future, Executive summary of What Matters Most: Teaching for America's Future. [On-line]. Available: http://www.tc.columbia.edu/~teachcomm/what.htm

Lankes, A. M. D. (1995, December). Electronic portfolios: A new idea in assessment. ERIC Digest EDO-IR-95-9. [On-line]. Available: http://ericir.syr.edu/ithome/digests/portfolio.html

Lapp, D., Flood, J., & Lungren, L. (1995). Strategies for gaining access to the information superhighway: Off the side street and on to the main road. The Reading Teacher, 48, 5, 432-436.

Larimer, R. E. II. (1998, April 21). Commonly asked interview questions. [On-line]. Available: http://oak.cats.ohiou.edu/~rl228095/esp/interview/index.html

MacGinitie, W. H. (1993). Some limits of assessment. Journal of Reading, 36, 7, 556-59.

McFadden, J. J. (1994). Casting portfolios across the curriculum to encourage reflection. In S. O. Smyser, (Ed.), Encouraging reflection through portfolios (pp. 83-103). Proceedings of the National Conference on Linking Liberal Arts and Teacher Education. San Diego, CA. Sponsored by Rockefeller Brothers and University of Redlands.

McLaughlin, M. & Vogt, M.E. (1996). Portfolios in teacher education. Newark, DE: International Reading Association.

Murnane, Y. (1994). Portfolio use in higher education: A primer. In S. O. Smyser, (Ed.), Encouraging reflection through portfolios (pp. 73-82). Proceedings of the National Conference on Linking Liberal Arts and Teacher Education. San Diego, CA. Sponsored by Rockefeller Brothers and University of Redlands.

National Board for Professional Teaching Standards. (1997). [On-line]. Available: http://www.nbpts.org/nbpts/standards/intro.html

National Commission on Teaching and America's Future. (1998, Aprilo 11). [On-line]. Available: http://222.tc.columbia.edu/!teachcomm/what.htm

Paris, S. G. & Ayres, L. R. (1994). Becoming reflective students and teachers with portfolio and authentic assessment. Washington, DC: American Psychological Association.

Porter, C. & Cleland, J. (1995). The portfolio as a learning strategy. Portsmouth, NH: Boynton/Cook Publishers.

Ramlow, M. E. (1998). The personnel evaluation standards. American Evaluation Association. [On-line]. Available: http://www.eval.org/EvaluationDocuments/perseval.html

Roeder, P. E. (1994). Subject matter assessment of preservice elementary teachers: The San Diego State University Liberal Studies Assessment Portfolio. In S. O. Smyser, (Ed.), Encouraging reflection through portfolios (pp. 34-49). Proceedings of the National Conference on Linking Liberal Arts and Teacher Education. San Diego, CA. Sponsored by Rockefeller Brothers and University of Redlands.

Ross, J. (1997, May 23) What is a teaching portfolio? [On-line]. Available: http://tier.net/schools/portfol.htm

Rousculp, E. E. & Maring, G. H. (1992). Portfolios for a community of learners. Journal of Reading, 35, 5, 378-85.

Santa, C. M. & Santa, J. L. (1995). Teacher as researcher. Journal of Reading Behavior, 27, 3, 439-51.

Smith, E. M. (1992). Answering the voices in my head: Students and teachers can make a difference. The Reading Teacher, 45, 6, 424-27.

Smyser, S. O., (Ed.). (1994, October). Encouraging reflection through portfolios. Proceedings of the National Conference on Linking Liberal Arts and Teacher Education. San Diego, CA. Sponsored by Rockefeller Brothers and University of Redlands.

Stahle, D. L. & Mitchell, J. P. (1993). Portfolio assessment in college methods courses: Practicing what we preach. Journal of Reading, 36, 7, 538-42.

Supovitz, J. A. (1997, November 5). From multiple-choice to multiple-choices. Education Week on the Web. [On-line]. Available: http://www.edweek.org/htbin/fastweb?getdo...YWORDS%26OR%26%28portfolio%26standards%29

Swanson, D. B., Norman, G. R., & Linn, R. L. (1995). Performance-based assessment: Lessons from the health professions. Educational Researcher, 24, 4, 5-11, 35.

Teaching as a profession. (1997). Education Week on the Web. [On-line]. Available: http://www.edweek.org/context/topics/teaching.htm.

Tierney, R. J., Carter, M. A., & Desai, L. E. (1991). Portfolio assessment in the reading-writing classroom. Norwood, MA: Christopher Gordon.

Valencia, S. (1990). A portfolio approach to classroom reading assessment: The whys, whats, and hows. The Reading Teacher, 43, 4, 338-40.

Valeri-Gold, M., Olson, J. R., & Deming, M. P. (1992). Portfolios: Collaborative authentic assessment opportunities for college developmental learners. Journal of Reading, 35, 4, 298-305.

Wagner, C. L., Brock, D. R. & Agnew, A. T. (1994). Developing literacy portfolios in teacher education course. Journal of Reading, 37, 8, 668-75.

Wilcox, B. L. (1996). Smart portfolios for teachers in training. Journal of Adolescent and Adult Literacy, 40, 3, 172-179.

Wilcox, B. L. (1997). The teacher's portfolio: An essential tool for professional development. The Reading Teacher, 51, 2, 170-73.

Wolf, K. & Siu-Runyan, Y. (1996). Portfolio purposes and possibilities. Journal of Adolescent and Adult Literacy, 40, 1, 30-37.

Worcester, T. (1998, April 18). What to include in electronic portfolios. [On-line]. Available: http://www.sv400.k12.ks.us/port/what.html

Young, J. P., Mathews, S. R., Kietzmann, A. M., & Westerfield, T. (1997). Getting disenchanted adolescents to participate in school literacy activities: Portfolio conferences. Journal of Adolescent and Adult Literacy, 40, 5, 348-60.